D0256035

100 THINGS YOU WILL NEVER DO

///// CAUTiON /////

The information in this book is designed to entertain only and is not intended as a practical guide for undertaking the pursuits described. Many of the activities presented are highly dangerous and involve serious risk of injury or death; they should not be attempted under any circumstances. Nothing in this book should be construed as advice or recommendation to undertake any of the activities. The author and publishers expressly disclaim any responsibility for any adverse effects arising from the use or application of the information contained herein.

100 THINGS YOU WILL NEVER DO

AND HOW TO ACHIEVE THE IMPOSSIBLE

DANIEL SMITH

Quercus

Contents

Introduction

'Impossible is a word to be found only in the dictionary of fools,' said Napoleon Bonaparte, a man not known for putting constraints upon himself. Of course, his plans for world domination did not end quite as he might have hoped, but there can be no knocking his ambition. The casual reader about to embark on a journey through this book could do much worse than familiarize themselves with the Little General's bon mots above – the refusal to accept failure, the desire to push oneself to the limit, the enthusiastic embracing of a life without boundaries. So steady your nerve, don the bicorne hat of destiny and prepare to take on challenges you never thought possible.

Over the pages that follow are a hundred activities that the average man or woman in the street is unlikely to ever attempt – unlikely, in some cases, to ever even want to attempt. Nonetheless, a good many of them are more achievable than you might imagine, given the odd compromise and bit of lateral thinking. Some probe at the very boundaries of science, while others will appeal to thrill-seekers, people who wish to examine their personal limits and those who are simply in search of new experiences.

But first, a word of warning. Several entries, you will soon realize, are here for pure reading entertainment and shouldn't be considered as a challenge to take up in the real world. A few are so utterly reckless that no one in their right mind would want to try them anyway. For instance, while Russian roulette might make for a dramatic scene in *The Deer Hunter*, in real life it is a game for the terminally stupid. Nor is it being suggested that you might like to try to steal the *Mona Lisa* – and hopefully you will never be in the position where you need to escape from Alcatraz. Similarly, only a fool would consider wrestling an alligator anywhere but in the relative safety of their imagination.

However, what these hundred entries illustrate is that very little in this world is utterly un-doable.

Whether it is a case of nudging against the basic laws of science and nature or merely stepping beyond our personal limits, even that which we consider impossible may be reassigned as 'eminently achievable' (even if simultaneously retaining the labels of 'distinctly improbable' and 'highly inadvisable' too).

Most of these activities are not the sort of thing you can undertake on a whim in the morning and master by sunset. Each requires a dedication to the cause, a steely focus and in most cases a determination to learn skills you probably never knew you had. But as the writer and philosopher George Santayana once noted: 'The Difficult is that which can be done immediately; the Impossible that which takes a little longer.'

What this book is *not* is any kind of comprehensive instructional guide to tell you everything you need to know to complete each challenge. If you plan to undertake any of them, it is essential that you seek out expert advice and guidance on how to prepare for and achieve them. Make yourself aware of any risks and be sure to keep within the law! In certain cases, you may also want to double-check that your life insurance premiums are up to date.

Those who feel they lack the necessary vim and vigour to take up the gauntlet should remember the

words of Helen Keller: 'Optimism is the faith that leads to achievement. Nothing can be done without hope and confidence.'

Few people who have ever lived could rival Keller's track record of achieving that which had seemed all but impossible. Born in 1880, she was not yet two years old when she contracted an illness (perhaps meningitis or scarlet fever) that left her blind and deaf and, apparently, without the vital tools to communicate with the world. However, thanks in no small part to the tireless efforts of her companion and teacher Anne Sullivan, Keller not only learned to communicate, but became one of the most notable campaigning figures of her age. In 1904 she became the first deaf-blind person to receive a Bachelor of Arts degree, when she graduated from Radcliffe College in Cambridge, Massachusetts. She went on to serve as a fearless spokeswoman for, among others, the disabled, workers, pacifists, suffragists and the family planning movement. She also published twelve books in her lifetime, befriending writers, celebrities, industrialists and presidents along the way for good measure. So it seems fitting to leave the final word to Keller, a woman who overcame enormous challenges to achieve extraordinary things: 'Life is either a daring adventure or nothing at all.'

1 Score in a World Cup final

WHAT IT IS Hitting the back of the net on the biggest stage imaginable
WHY YOU WON'T DO IT In a match played once every four years and averaging 1.5 goals per game since 1990, few ever get the chance

Today, soccer is *the* global game, and it offers no greater glory than scoring a goal in the World Cup final. If you hit the net in the biggest game of them all, you'll never have to buy a drink again. So lace up those golden boots, and prepare for immortality.

Your first step is to become good enough so that your national coach plays you – and while not all World Cup goalscorers play as strikers, this position traditionally offers the most opportunity for glory.

You should be fit, speedy and physically robust. Develop the mythical 'good first touch' that allows you to immediately bring the ball under control. Master heading the ball, and shooting with both feet, and definitely make sure you can take penalties – some great players, and indeed entire teams, have been found wanting in this department (for instance, Italy's Roberto Baggio, the best player in the world at the time, famously missed in the 1994 World Cup final). Above all, don't be a shrinking violet – no great striker ever is.

Having thus reached international standard, what else should you consider? Choose your country wisely – if your passport dictates that you play for Tonga or the Faroe Islands, kiss goodbye to your World Cup dream. Thirty-two countries qualify for the finals from an initial field of more than 200 national teams. Once at the finals, a country must fight its way through a mini league, with 16 teams progressing to a knockout format comprising a second round, quarter-finals, semi-finals and *the* final. Since the first final in 1934, only 12 countries have appeared in the showcase match, and it's extremely rare for a new nation to break into that exclusive gang.

Once you've reached the final, hold your nerve. Not only will there be tens of thousands of fans in the stadium, but you can also expect a TV audience in excess of 700 million. You will not get many chances, so make the most of anything that falls to you – few World Cup final goals are things of beauty.

Prepare a suitable celebration for your moment of glory – these days celebrating a goal involves more choreography than you'll see at a disco convention. And remember to wear your smartest pants – Brazilian legend Jairzinho recalls being stripped to his underwear by enthusiastic fans at the end of the 1970 final!

2 Base jump from the Burj Khalifa

WHAT IT IS A chance to check out Newton's theories from the top of the world's tallest building
WHY YOU WON'T DO IT The ground is unforgiving and canvas a flimsy fabric to which to trust your life

Base jumping is the sport of jumping with a parachute from a fixed point – in effect, it's a radically truncated form of skydiving. The word 'BASE' itself is an acronym standing for the various categories of fixed object: buildings, antennae, spans (bridges) and earth (more often than not, cliffs). So how about trying it from the tallest building in the world?

As you could probably guess, base jumping is dangerous, foolhardy and, in a great many places, illegal. One early exponent was Franz Reichelt, an Austrian-born French tailor who launched himself from the top of the Eiffel Tower in 1912 in order to test his newly invented 'parachute coat'. Reichelt's aims were noble – he hoped that his suit would save aviators who were unexpectedly forced to bail out of their aircraft – and the authorities had granted permission for his test on the assumption that Reichelt would be using a dummy. However, showing impressive but unwarranted faith in his own invention, the 'Flying Tailor' insisted he would test the device himself, and paid the price when his parachute failed to deploy and he died on impact.

Reichelt's lesson seems to have discouraged others from following in his footsteps for more than half a century, and by the time the idea was resurrected as a modern 'extreme sport' in the late 1970s, parachute technology had changed almost beyond recognition.

The highest jump from a building so far was achieved in 2010 by Omar Al Hegelan and Nasr Al Niyadi, when they plummeted from the Burj Khalifa skyscraper in Dubai, the tallest man-made structure in the world at 828 metres (2,717 ft). Their jump involved an impressive ten seconds of free fall before their parachutes activated. They survived, but the sport's estimated death rate is staggering – ultimately accounting for around one in sixty participants. No one is going to better Al Hegelan and Al Niyadi's record until someone builds a taller tower, but you could at least try to equal it.

You'll need to undertake specialist training with an experienced base jumper and, meanwhile, build up your experience of normal skydiving. (No one said this would be easy.) On average, a base jumper will have completed around a hundred 'ordinary' skydives before attempting his or her first jump. In time, your trainer will become a trusted mentor who can let you know when you're ready to take the next step.

DON'T LOOK DOWN *When it opened in 2010, the Burj Khalifa in Dubai officially became the world's tallest building. Rising almost 830 metres (2,720 ft) into the sky, its chief architect was Adrian Smith of Chicago firm Skidmore, Owings and Merrill. Construction of the 163 floors cost a total of US$1.5 billion, but the project had to be bailed out with money from Abu Dhabi following the global financial crisis.*

Buy your tickets for Dubai (returns if you're feeling lucky), and check your life insurance premiums are up to date (if they'll even cover you for this sort of thing).You'd also better ask the owners for permission to jump: the 2010 jump was carried out with the blessing of the Dubai authorities, but two years previously (before the official opening), a Briton and a Frenchman disguised as engineers snuck into the building and launched themselves from a balcony between the 150th and 160th floors.

Do your homework – go and see exactly where you'll be jumping from and keep a special lookout for any unexpected impediments or obstacles.

On the day of your jump, ensure your specially made base-jumping parachute (typical price, US$1200–$1500) is properly packed. Base jumpers favour the ram-air parachute – a rectangular design that allows for greater control of speed and direction. Because of the shortage of time, some jumpers opt to open their pilot chute (the one that pulls the main chute open) manually, rather than with a ripcord. You should just about have time enough to employ a slider that opens the parachute slowly to avoid troublesome tangled lines and violent jolts.

Check your back-up parachute too – you'll have just about have enough time to deploy it in an emergency, For jumps below 600 metres (2,000 ft), there's no point in a back-up as by the time your main chute has failed, you'll already be intimately familiar with the ground. Jumpers from lower heights instead tend to employ a slightly larger pilot chute, which ensures the main chute not only opens more quickly, but is also more effective at the lower velocities generated by a shorter jump.

Take one last look for any new obstacles on the ground below, and step out into the unknown. Be sure to get some distance between you and the side of the building – hitting the side of the tower could be just as lethal as hitting the ground. Release the pilot chute at around 600 metres (2,000 ft) and steer yourself to a safe landing. Just don't forget to dodge any window cleaners you pass on the way down – it's a non-stop job and it takes a team of 36 workers up to four months to clean all of the tower's windows.

3 Dine on puffer fish

WHAT IT IS A delicacy from the deep that takes years of experience to prepare safely

WHY YOU WON'T DO IT Why we might talk about food that is 'to die for', do you really want to test out the theory?

Have you grown tired of beans on toast? Do you feel ready for a new culinary adventure? Then look no further than the puffer fish or *fugu*. This toxic little sea monster is found in tropical seas around the world, and if carelessly prepared, could leave you facing a long and painful death.

Belonging to the family of fish known as Tetraodontidae, the puffer fish's Japanese name literally translates as 'river pig'. With a name like that, as you might guess, it's not much to look at. But its aesthetics are the least of your problems. What you really have to be worried about is the high levels of the poison tetrodotoxin it contains – enough to see off 30 adult humans. So maybe you should consider whether you really need to try puffer fish? A nice bit of smoked salmon or dover sole can fill an empty belly just as well.

But if you're still game, you will probably want to eat the fish in its spiritual homeland of Japan. Here, it has been considered a delicacy for more than two millennia. It is also popular in South Korea, but cannot be sold legally in the European Union. Some 17 restaurants across the United States have a legal certificate allowing them to serve it, of which 12 are in New York.

The fish can be served in several different forms. In the classic dish sashimi, it is sliced so thinly that it becomes translucent. Otherwise you might have it deep-fried, in a salad or a stew. The fins can also be baked, while some cooks claim that the roe (egg mass) is most tasty. Do not consider trying to cook the fish yourself. It must be prepared by trained professionals. Eager amateurs have a strong chance of killing themselves, partly because the poison is not affected by the heating process – the toxic areas of the fish must be physically cut out.

In Japan, chefs have been required to have a licence to sell and prepare the fish since 1958. To get their licence they must pass an exacting series of tests after completing a three-year apprenticeship. It includes a written component, a fish identification exercise and a practical cooking test, finishing with a tasting. Chefs must be able to identify and cleanly remove organs, eyes and other poisonous parts. Worryingly, the pass rate is just 35 per cent – though fortunately most of the other 65 per cent seem to flunk on the

FISH DISH *The puffer fish might not be the most attractive of dining companions, but it is among the most highly prized. There are some 120 species of puffer, almost exclusively found in the tropics and usually in inshore waters. Opposite, a highly trained chef carefully prepares a fugu for the plate.*

written or preparation parts rather than during the tasting.

If you're worried that you might have been poisoned, there are some early symptoms to be aware of. These include tingling lips and tongue. You might also feel headachy, nauseous, tired, dizzy and short of breath. Tetrodotoxin attacks the nervous system and can cause paralysis. However, it does not directly affect the brain, so those afflicted can suffer an agonizing physical shut-down, remaining conscious but unable to communicate. In a worst case scenario, the victim will die as a result of asphyxiation.

There is no known antidote to counter the poison. However, treatment includes emptying the patient's stomach, giving him or her activated charcoal to try to neutralize the toxin, and putting them on a life support machine until the poison dissipates.

A decade-long study of poisonings in Japan up to 2006 recorded an average of 20–44 cases per year. About 7 per cent of those resulted in fatalities. The *Torafugu* (tiger blowfish) is the most prized and most poisonous of all the puffer fish species, with a particularly toxic liver. In 1975, one of Japan's most beloved actors, Bandō Mitsugorō VIII, died after reputedly consuming an excessive quantity of puffer liver. By 1984, it became illegal to serve the liver even in Japan.

For those not sure they're prepared to risk their lives for the sake of a fish supper, there is some hope. Some academics believe that the tetrodotoxin is produced by the puffer fish's digestive system, so attempts to artifically produce a non-poisonous (but equally delicious) breed of puffer fish through carefully regulated food intake are currently underway.

4 Free dive

WHAT IT IS Exploring the deep blue sea without the aid of breathing apparatus **WHY YOU WON'T DO IT** You will put your body under stresses you have no right to survive

Free diving is the art of diving without breathing equipment, relying entirely on the diver's ability to hold their breath. Known as competitive apnea when performed as a modern sport, it has been practised since ancient times by divers in search of food, shells, sponges and pearls. Today, the world's greatest free divers are able to hold their breath for up to nine minutes underwater.

Before attempting to free dive, go and get professional training. Not only will it keep you safer, it will increase your enjoyment. Moderate training can allow even a relative novice to hold their breath for up to 45 seconds – long enough to dive to 10 metres (33 ft) and enjoy visions of the underwater world unavailable to recreational snorkellers. You'll actually find you can do a lot of your training on land – for instance, take a deep breath and see how far you can walk. Through repetition, you will soon see improvements in your ability to safely hold your breath. Yoga is also recommended for developing breathing control.

Make sure you are in good health before you dive. Ensure that you are warm and relaxed before going in, and don't get in the water if you are carrying an injury or if you are suffering a heavy cold or respiratory illness. Don't launch straight into a dive but float on the water's surface in order to relax, bringing your heart rate down. When you're ready, take a breath and hold it as you plunge down through the water, keeping your legs vertical. To propel yourself down, kick your legs in short, controlled strokes. Your instinct may be to make violent movements, particularly if you are panicking, but this will only use up extra energy and breath. Slow and deliberate movement is far more economical.

Equalize the pressure in your ears by pinching your nose and blowing through your nostrils. This will stop your ears from rupturing as the pressure from the surrounding water increases. The greatest risk is a syndrome known as 'shallow water blackout' (caused by falling levels of carbon dioxide in your bloodstream) that can lead to fainting without warning – something that can have tragic consequences. This is why you should always dive with a companion, but it's well worth investing in a safety vest that uses an automatic timer to inflate and refloat you back to the surface if you encounter problems. When you're ready to ascend, do so slowly and smoothly to eke out your lungful of breath for the maximum time.

5 Ride in a camel race

WHAT IT IS Navigating a 'ship of the desert' between points A and B faster than your rivals
WHY YOU WON'T DO IT This is a challenge guaranteed to give you the hump

Camels can reach speeds of up to 64 kilometres per hour (40 mph) during sprints, and can maintain a steady 40 kilometres per hour (25 mph) over much longer distances. Phenomenally popular throughout much of the Middle East, in India, Pakistan, Mongolia and also Australia, camel racing has become big business. It could be the perfect sport for you – if you don't mind a slightly bumpy ride.

Some camel races can leave winning owners extremely wealthy and there's a social scene to rival anything you'll see in horseracing. Indeed, it is said that Sheikh Zayed, a former president of the United Arab Emirates, was such a fan that he kept a personal stable of 14,000 camels with a staff of 9,000 to look after them. With all that oil wealth sloshing around, it's no surprise there's lots of money at stake – in 2010 one breeding female with an impressive racing heritage sold for US$2.45 million.

Some of the biggest race meets in Australia are in July and August, while the racing season across the Middle East runs from late October to early April. Race distances can be anything from 2 to 10 kilometres (1.2 to 6 miles), and fields can vary from as few as six camels up to as many as 75. As you might imagine, a race containing dozens of moody camels is no place for faint hearts or weak wills. As with horseracing, the general rule is the lighter you are the better. However, the professional sport has been besieged by allegations of human rights abuses

relating to underage jockeys. It has been known for children as young as six to be entered into races so that the load on the camel is as light as possible. However, the rules have now been tightened in the face of international consternation, and today jockeys are generally required to be at least 15 years old and to weigh more than 45 kilograms (99 lb).

Perhaps in response to this, in recent years some camel owners have attempted to do away with jockeys altogether, preferring to use saddle-mounted robots instead – it's not worth wasting your time trying to find a ride with an owner who will only consider you if you can be remote controlled.

A racing camel comes into its prime when it is two or three years old. Most tend to be female, because they are slightly less temperamental than their male counterparts. However, even they can be moody and unpredictable. They are not averse to spitting and kicking and, *in extremis*, can give a nasty bite. Therefore, always treat your camel

ROBOT WARS *Lighter, easier to look after and less likely to be full of their own opinions, it is perhaps little surprise that several leading owners of racing camels have invested in robots as an alternative to human jockeys. Best of all, if the camel triumphs the owner doesn't have to share his winnings.*

respectfully, calmly and confidently. If you panic, it will too, and that's a real recipe for trouble.

A standing camel is quite a beast, so riders mount when they are lying down. There is likely to be a ledge or lip on the camel's saddle – put one of your legs onto it, and gently swing your other leg across the camel's hump. Grip the saddle firmly with your knees and hang on tight – when a camel stands up, it leans first forwards, then backwards, and these are the prime moments for you to fall off. Try to tilt your own body in the opposite direction to the camel's lean to give you as much stability as possible.

Fortunately, there aren't any mechanical stalls to worry about – the start of these long-distance races is signalled by the lifting of a long, rope-like barrier. Try to remain as relaxed as possible. Not only will this keep the camel calm, but it will also help you maintain the flexibility of movement you'll need to stay upright as your camel takes off like a rocket. As in horseracing, you have a whip to encourage your mount. You'll also need goggles to protect your eyes, but may still have trouble seeing through the huge dust clouds created by stampeding hooves on desert ground.

Finally, watch out for bad sportsmanship – with the potential rewards getting ever larger, animals that place in big races are routinely drug-tested. In addition, there have been scandals over the use of 'whips' that deliver an electric shock to make the camels go faster. Hang on and good luck!

6 Trek to the South Pole

WHAT IT IS Retracing the routes of some of history's most legendary explorers
WHY YOU WON'T DO IT Modern technology gives you a greater chance of survival than ever before but you'll still be pushed to your limits

The desire to reach the South Pole cost the lives of many intrepid explorers before a team led by Roald Amundsen planted the Norwegian flag there in 1911. The most southerly point on planet Earth is subject to extremes of weather and presents unique challenges – it's not a trip to be undertaken lightly, but if planned with precision it will likely be the journey of your life.

After the expeditions of Amundsen and the ill-fated Robert Falcon Scott, it was to be a further 45 years before man returned to the South Pole, and even today it remains one of the most inaccessible and hostile places on Earth. Despite this, sizeable numbers of adventurers do now complete the trip, so if you want to take up the challenge, do your homework beforehand. There are now several companies that offer guided trips. They may cost a lot, but you are paying in part for their extensive experience and your own peace of mind.

Make sure you are physically capable of making the trip. You'll be covering long distances, hauling heavy sleds in extreme cold, so get a comprehensive medical to see if you're up to it. You'll also need to dress for the occasion, wearing at least three layers at all times:
• A layer of thermal underwear and undershirts.
• A middle layer consisting of fleeces or warm trousers and jackets.
• An outer layer of water- and windproof jacket and trousers.

Frostbite is a constant threat, so don a balaclava and/or hat, light inner gloves and a pair of waterproof outer gloves, plus toe warmers and leg and arm gauntlets. Quality UV-protection sunglasses will help ward off snow-blindness, while steel-toed waterproof boots with good grip and support around the ankle are essential in Antarctic conditions.

Under the advice of your tour guides, stock up on essential high-energy foods. Your body will scream out for regular fuel in such hostile circumstances, and it's estimated that a man hauling his sled for a day will use up 6,500 calories. Even if you use dog sledges, you can still expect to burn through 5,000 calories.

A classic itinerary might last 60 or more days and begin with a meet-up in Chile for a day of pre-trek checks. From there, you'll be flown to the Union Glacier base camp, a journey of four and a half hours. You will spend a couple of days here, practising routines and ensuring everyone and everything is good to go,

SPORT AND LEISURE

INTO THE UNKNOWN *The image opposite is an atmospheric shot taken during Robert Scott's ill-starred expedition to the South Pole in 1911–12. Intrepid modern explorers (above) can call upon experienced heads and all the latest technology, but the trip remains a formidable challenge.*

before flying to Hercules Inlet, on the southwest edge of the Ronne Ice Shelf. It's here that the hard work begins.

Dragging your laden sledge, you have 1,175 kilometres (730 miles) to cover. You will climb from sea level to more than 3,300 metres (10,800 ft) during the journey, encountering temperatures of -40°C (-40°F) and a variety of terrains.

As you ski the last few kilometres you will spy the welcoming buildings of the US Amundsen-Scott South Pole Station, a research centre that's well worth exploring on your arrival (though perhaps after a short rest). Indeed, if you

fancy a longer stay, you might consider applying for a job at the station – though competition for vacancies is fierce.

The Ceremonial South Pole offers photo opportunities for the end of your trip, complete with a small monument and assorted flags. However, you should be aware that the Geographic South Pole is a short distance further on – be sure to visit both sites as the chances are you won't be back here any time soon.

If you're feeling brave enough to make the trip under your own steam, consider following in the ski tracks of Arved Fuchs and Reinhold Messner, who in 1989 became the first people to cross Antarctica via the South Pole without the aid of beast or machine. The fastest trip to the pole from the ocean, meanwhile, was completed in a little over 24 days by a Norwegian, Christian Eide, in 2011.

Become an Olympic champion

WHAT IT IS Proving you're peerless at the greatest sporting event on Earth
WHY YOU WON'T DO IT Because there aren't many gold medals to go round

Baron Pierre de Coubertin founded the modern Olympics in 1896. Ever since, winning Olympic gold has been the dream of sportsmen and women throughout the world. To have any hope of joining this exclusive club requires a mix of genetic and physiological good fortune, a nurturing environment where your talent can be spotted and developed, huge amounts of determination and a dose of good luck.

Unfortunately, the first thing you need is something you have no control over – good genes. There's no doubt about it, some of us are less physiologically suited to great sporting attainment than others. Coming from a wealthy country also helps your chances. At the 2008 Beijing Games, the leading nations were China, the USA, Russia, Great Britain, Germany and Australia – all are major economies with plenty of resources to throw at developing their Olympic athletes.

Do not lose all hope if you come from a less wealthy nation, though. Plenty of countries buck the trend. Cuba has been phenomenally strong in the boxing ring over the years while Kenya and Ethiopia have dominated long-distance running for decades. Talent will out, and medal tables adjusted to take account of GDP tend to look very different.

Assuming you do have an innate talent, identify the sport you're best suited to early. There are honourable exceptions (British sportswoman Rebecca Romero won medals at consecutive Olympics for rowing in 2004 and then cycling in 2008) but most champions do not come to a sport late. The London 2012 Games encompassed some 300 events across 26 sports, so hopefully there is something for everyone.

From school age onwards, you'll need to set yourself clear, realistic and achievable goals, and maintain your hunger. Seek out coaches who can help you improve, and compete against rivals who will drive you on (even if you frequently lose to them). Learn to deal with these knockbacks, as there will be plenty. You can rely on experiencing injury, unexpected defeats, financial pressures and relationship stresses. How you deal with them is critical and being surrounded by supportive friends and families is a great boon.

Study the history of your chosen discipline. What can you learn from the greats of the past? Constantly strive to improve. If your technique is wonderful, work on your endurance or improve your psychology. The greatest competitors

GOLDEN BOY *Arguably the greatest sprinter who ever lived, Usain Bolt of Jamaica (seen here taking the bend in the 200 metres) dominated the individual and relay sprint events at both the 2008 and 2012 Olympic Games, securing himself a place among the pantheon of Olympic greats.*

do not focus their training only on their strengths but look to overcome any weaknesses too.

To achieve Olympic standard, you can expect to train for between three and nine hours every day, depending on your sport, but most top sports people acknowledge that you can be as fine a physical specimen as is possible but your mind must be right too. Certainly at the top end of sports, where the difference between victory and defeat might be fractions of a second or a question of millimetres, mentality can make all the difference. Consider employing a sports psychologist: with help, you should be able to increase your ability to focus, maintain self-discipline, cope with stress and learn when to relax and wind down.

Being a competitor is expensive. Aside from the cost of equipment and everyday living, you will face expensive bills for travel, coaches, physios, nutritionists and psychologists. Unless you are one of the very few who secures commercial sponsorship, you will need to approach your national Olympic funding body and

can expect to live quite humbly during your quest for glory.

You will, of course, need to achieve Olympic qualification standards. For instance, in athletics you must reach either the A or B standards set by the International Association of Athletics Federations. Each nation may put forward up to three athletes who achieve the higher A standard, and an additional one at the B standard. Qualification periods vary but generally cover a year to 18 months before the Games.

All this work requires almost unearthly amounts of commitment. In 1996 after securing a gold medal at a fourth consecutive Olympics, Olympic rower Steve Redgrave announced that anyone who saw him in a boat again had permission to shoot him. Yet four years later in Sydney, Redgrave won his fifth gold at the age of 38. This is the sort of devotion, passion and possible streak of insanity that you must aspire to. Believe you can be the champion – somebody will have that gold medal around their neck, so why shouldn't it be you?

8 Sail around the world

WHAT IT IS Following in the footsteps of Ferdinand Magellan
WHY YOU WON'T DO IT Only the best mariners armed with plenty of time and money even stand a chance

Circumnavigating the globe has always been the ultimate sailing challenge, and since Ferdinand Magellan proved it was possible in the 16th century, many others have followed in his wake. These days it remains a true test, but it's one that can be conquered if you approach it the right way.

Your first job is to decide exactly why you want to sail around the world. Do you want to get round as quickly as possible, perhaps even breaking a record, or do you want to go at a more leisurely place, taking in some of the wondrous sights and experiences on offer en route? Your decision will affect how long you expect to be away, what sort of boat you choose, what supplies to take and which skills to brush up on, as well as who you will have as crew.

In general (though rules vary if you're sailing competitively), a circumnavigation should see you pass through every line of longitude, cover a distance at least equal to the world's circumference (some 40,075 kilometres or 24,901 miles), and pass a pair of antipodal points (that is to say, points directly opposite each other on the globe). A racing route usually loops around the perilous tips of South America and Southern Africa, testing even the best sailors to their limits. So let's assume you are happy to take a more leisurely route, avoiding these dangerous corners and passing through the shortcuts of the Panama and Suez Canals instead.

Before even considering a trip, you should be an experienced sailor, ideally with at least two years under your belt. Gather as much expert advice as you can in making your preparations. Read books, attend sailing fairs and speak to those who have already done it and survived to tell the tale.

Plan the route in minute detail: research prevailing wind patterns, ocean currents, average temperatures and other climate conditions, and factor in considerations including expenses (for one thing, you'll be charged for access to both canals), suitable stopovers for repairs and supplies, and any particular tourist spots you would like to visit!

Avoid anything that will take you into geopolitically dangerous environments and beware of emerging risks – for instance, the coast of Somalia has long been tormented by violent acts of piracy so aim to steer clear. In

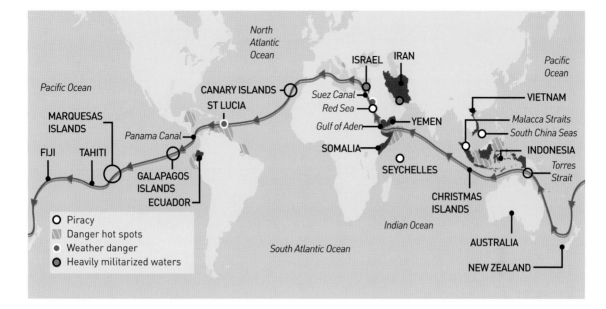

The map includes the following labels:

North Atlantic Ocean
Pacific Ocean
Pacific Ocean
ISRAEL
IRAN
CANARY ISLANDS
ST LUCIA
Suez Canal
Red Sea
Gulf of Aden
YEMEN
VIETNAM
Malacca Straits
South China Seas
MARQUESAS ISLANDS
Panama Canal
SOMALIA
INDONESIA
Torres Strait
FIJI
TAHITI
GALAPAGOS ISLANDS
ECUADOR
SEYCHELLES
CHRISTMAS ISLANDS
Indian Ocean
South Atlantic Ocean
AUSTRALIA
NEW ZEALAND

○ Piracy
▧ Danger hot spots
● Weather danger
◉ Heavily militarized waters

THE HARD WAY, OR THE TOURIST ROUTE? *While round the world racing yachts such as the one shown opposite must fight the rough seas around Cape Horn and the Cape of Good Hope, even the most ambitious round-the-world tourists take advantage of shortcuts offered by the Panama and Suez Canals. Despite this, as the map above illustrates, there are still many hazards to avoid.*

addition, make sure that your passport is up to date, that you have visas for any countries that require them, and that you have a sound understanding of maritime law.

Choose your vessel carefully. A wooden boat might seem romantic, but it is likely to provide you with many more practical problems than one made from metal or fibreglass, and will also be more expensive to insure as a result. For two people, a 12-metre (40-ft) boat is ideal – big enough to offer comfort but small enough for one person to sail if the other is incapacitated.

Learn all that you can about how the boat works so that you are capable of making running repairs. Make sure it is installed with GPS and communication systems, an autopilot, battery chargers and facilities to purify water. While

there is much technology to assist you in navigation, make sure that you can confidently read a nautical chart and work out your position from the stars alone. These are old but timeless skills, and in certain circumstances they might just save your life.

Give yourself at least a year of sailing to finish the trip. This means that you'll need to get your finances in good order before you go. Make sure you have comprehensive health and travel insurance policies too. File your travel plans with friends or family – they will be invaluable in the event of an emergency.

You'll need to keep focused for the duration of the trip – no lounging about on deck! Check daily that the boat remains in good condition and that all on-board systems are working as they should do. If something goes amiss, dock for running repairs as soon as you can. Finally, pack some good books or films to keep you entertained during long days and nights on the sea. And don't forget to turn off the gas and cancel the milk before you leave.

9 Run the Marathon des Sables

WHAT IT IS The endurance event to top them all
WHY YOU WON'T DO IT Because multiple marathons in the desert are not most people's cup of tea

If you're bored of simple marathons and want a challenge on an entirely different plane, look no further than the Marathon des Sables, a six-day ultramarathon through the Sahara desert in southern Morocco. As the saying goes: 'Any idiot can run an ultramarathon but it takes a special kind of idiot to run the Marathon des Sables.'

First run in 1986, the race route takes in 251 kilometres (156 miles) – equivalent to almost six ordinary marathons. However, the stages are not of equal length – the shortest is a comparatively brief 21 kilometres (13 miles), while the longest is a gruelling 88.5 kilometres (55 miles). Little wonder it's widely regarded as the hardest foot race in the world, with two recorded fatalities among competitors over the years.

This is a race all about long preparation. Ideally, start thinking about your training schedule a good 18 months in advance – don't expect to be able to deal with the demands placed upon your body and spirit if you have only managed a couple of jogs around the local park in the build-up. It's not uncommon for the temperature to hover around 40 °C (104°F), so if you can get in some warm-weather training, it is highly recommended. A Legionnaire hat and a good sun block are also worth their weight in gold. The total cost of competing (including entry fee) is estimated at around US$5,000.

Decide whether you are aiming simply to finish, or whether you have a chance of competing at the front. The winner in 2011 won in just under 21 hours, maintaining a pace equivalent to running a normal marathon every three and a half hours. Speak to people who have competed and read about their experiences – there is no better way of finding out what lies ahead of you.

As well as building up fitness and speed, focus on preparing your feet – they'll need to be healthy, supple and resilient. The extreme heat causes feet to swell, so it is a good idea to run in trainers that are initially too big. Blisters are the main reason that runners have to drop out of the race, and the organizers have a specialist team on hand to treat foot problems. There is also a medical team ready to assess you at each checkpoint. If you suffer from 'runner's rash' on your thighs, invest in compression shorts. Don't think about using anti-chafing lubricants – sand has a habit of sticking to them, turning your inner thighs into sandpaper. Ouch!

Remember to pack your kit correctly. In total, it should weigh 6.4–15 kilograms (14–33 lb), including food but excluding water, and will be inspected by officials before you're allowed to run. You should include: an anti-venom pump (Morocco has 12 types of poisonous snakes and 10 types of scorpion); a compass; disinfectant; distress flares; a knife; a lighter; a signalling mirror and signal stick; salt tablets; a sleeping bag; spare safety pins; a survival blanket; a torch (with batteries); and a whistle.

Eat high-energy foods – an average male runner will burn in excess of 5,000 calories per day. And as if it needs to be said, keep yourself hydrated. You will be carrying some water supplies and there will be more available en route. Bear in mind that you need twice or even four times as much water to run a marathon distance in the desert as for a standard city marathon. This is another reason to stick to the staging posts – in 1994 an Italian runner became disorientated during a sandstorm and was lost for nine days. When he was eventually found, he had lost 14 kilograms (30 lb) in weight. Also beware of steep dunes and rocks. They are difficult to see in this environment, and have accounted for plenty of non-finishers over the years.

Finally, enjoy the camaraderie of competing. At the end of each day you'll be sleeping under open-sided canvas with seven stinky, aching but brilliant fellow runners. You will be building unique bonds so make the most of it. And when you finish, make time to put your feet up for a day or two!

INTENSE EXPERIENCE

The Marathon des Sables has more to offer than just sand – there's also rocky terrain waiting to twist ankles and bruise shins. At the end of each arduous day's racing, competitors spend the night together under canvas (left). For those who have the energy left, unique friendships can be forged among competitors testing themselves to their limits.

10 Race a cheetah

WHAT IT IS Testing your speed against the world's paciest mammal
WHY YOU WON'T DO IT Because four legs are better than two

The cheetah, found in Africa and the Middle East, is perhaps the most graceful of the big cats – and even if your name is Usain Bolt, your chances of claiming victory in a sprint are pretty slim. The fastest land mammal of them all, in most races it'll leave you eating its dust. But what can you do to at least make a contest of it?

Weighing between 36 and 64 kilograms (80 and 140 lb), and growing 115–135 centimetres (46–55 in) long, a full-grown cheetah is compact and elegant, with a long tail that provides incredible turning ability at high speeds, and paws with semi-retractable claws that act like racing tyres. They can reach a top speed of 121 kilometres per hour (75 mph), and can hit 97 kilometres per hour (60 mph) in less than three seconds – faster than a Ferrari 458 Italia. In contrast, a top sprinter can manage about 40 kilometres per hour (25 mph).

Assuming you have a basis of decent speed, the key to running even faster is twofold. Firstly you need to improve your cadence – the number of steps you take each second. Secondly, you need to maximize the speed you generate every time your feet come into contact with the ground.

As with any training, you should begin with a thorough warm-up and stretching routine. Spend time working on your core stability muscles (stomach, hips, pelvis and bum) since these are crucial to making the necessary adjustments to your running style.

Learn to run in a relaxed style. This means that your body focuses only on the muscles required to sprint and does not waste energy anywhere else: facial grimaces and tight shoulders don't help anyone to move quicker.

Run with your head held high, as if a puppeteer high overhead is tugging you upright. You're whole body should feel like it is being pulled towards the sky, and your head should stay still as you sprint, with your chin slightly down. Lean slightly forward as you run, though be sure to maintain balance at all times. Your arms, meanwhile, should swing so that your elbows are slightly ahead of the plane of your trunk, allowing for optimum knee lift.

Focus on 'dorsiflexion' of the ankle as your foot strikes the ground – this means

FOUR LEGS BETTER THAN TWO *In 2007 South Africa's flying Rugby Union winger Bryan Habana – the joint highest try-scorer in the history of the Rugby World Cup – raced a cheetah as part of a campaign to highlight the plight of the threatened species.*

pointing your toes up towards your shin, which stretches the calf so that you generate the greatest possible impact from the strike. Your foot should hit the ground moving slightly backwards, and when your heel comes up from the ground, it should rise to almost touch your backside, rather than extending backwards.

Don't be downhearted if none of this takes you closer to the cheetah – there's no loss of pride in losing an athletic contest to a different species. In 2007 the flying South African rugby union star, Bryan Habana, raced a cheetah in a 'man versus beast' contest and came a distant second. He still recovered to help his team win the Rugby World Cup later in the year.

The trick, perhaps, is to choose your contests better. In 2002 Tom Johnson beat a horse over an 80-kilometre

(50-mile) course in the desert of the United Arab Emirates by ten seconds, largely because the horse lost an hour by having to stop to take on food and water.

The US Olympic legend Jesse Owens, famous for his victories at the 1936 Berlin Olympics, was controversially left to make a living by racing against horses and dogs. (He would later comment, 'People said it was degrading for an Olympic champion to run against a horse but... you can't eat four gold medals.') Anyway, he regularly won, though some believed that his greatest successes were against highly strung thoroughbred animals that panicked at the sound of the starting gun. However, it's a brave person who tries to agitate a cheetah in an attempt at gamesmanship. A fraught big cat will give you more problems than you could imagine.

Ultimately, if you are in a real hurry you could jump in a car, get a train or book yourself a plane ticket – not options that are readily available to a cheetah. This might seem like a small victory, but it's probably the best chance you've got.

11 Become a hot-dog-eating champion

WHAT IT IS Finding out whether your eyes really are bigger than your belly
WHY YOU WON'T DO IT You haven't got the stomach for it

Of all the ways to prove yourself to the world, scoffing a ridiculous number of hot dogs in a race against the clock is surely one of the strangest. Today, though, speed eating is big business, and Nathan's Famous Fourth of July Hot Dog Eating Contest on Coney Island is the blue riband event, complete with a US$10,000 prize pot.

The Coney Island contest attracts TV audiences in excess of 1.5 million, and there is serious fame and fortune to be found as a speed-eating competitor throughout the USA and in Japan. At the highest level the 'sport' is governed by the International Federation of Competitive Eating (IFOCE), which seeks to expand its popularity and maintain standards of safety.

The current record for the Fourth of July competition stands at 68 hot dogs (sausage and bun!) consumed in 12 minutes. Contests are generally restricted to 8, 10, 12 or 15 minutes to avoid putting undue strain on the body and to keep the attention of spectators. This is a sport in which both men and women can compete – and indeed, two of the top ten speed eaters in recent years (sometimes charmingly referred to as 'gurgitators') have been women. A surprisingly comprehensive set of rules has been worked out over the years. First off, all competitors must be over 18. Dunking of food into water or other drinks to soften them is allowed, as is 'chipmunking' (when an eater crams as much food as possible into his or her mouth at the last second). To win, you will need to be highly coordinated so that you can grab, dunk and consume all at the same time. Vomiting during or for a set period after the contest results in immediate disqualification.

The best speed eaters undoubtedly train their stomachs to expand. However, this is not something to be undertaken lightly – artificially expanding your stomach can lead to permanent damage. The IFOCE does not support training at home – it insists that any such exercises should take place in a controlled environment, after consultation with your doctor and with a medic on hand.

Stuffing your face with food obviously causes weight gain so competitors should undertake regular exercise to ensure they stay trim. Some also chew gum in a bid to improve the flexibility of their jaw, and one leading eater declared that his training had resulted in an arthritic jaw!

12 Drink a bottle of 1787 Château Lafite

WHAT IT IS Some of the most expensive wine in the world
WHY YOU WON'T DO IT Who wants to spend a fortune on a tipple that's probably corked by now?

In 1985, a bottle of 1787 Château Lafite was sold at auction by Christie's for a cool US$160,000, making it the most expensive standard bottle of wine in history. If you pride yourself on knowing your Sauvignon Blanc from your Shiraz, you might lust after a bottle of this choice vintage – but you probably wouldn't want to drink it.

The record-breaking bottle was bought by Christopher Forbes, a son of the famous *Forbes Magazine* dynasty. As a wine collector, he was particularly drawn to the bottle because it was etched with the three letters 'Th.J'. This, it was reported, was proof that the wine came from the collection of the USA's third president and one of its founding fathers, Thomas Jefferson.

Jefferson served a stint as ambassador to France and took the opportunity to develop his taste for fine wine. And they don't come any finer than those from the vineyards of Château Lafite, near the village of Paulliac in the Médoc region northwest of Bordeaux. The Château made its name in the early 18th century thanks to the winemaking prowess of its owner, Nicolas-Alexandre, the marquis de Ségur, and his shrewd stroke of marketing genius in introducing his wines to the French royal court. Since the 19th century it has been owned by the powerful Rothschild family, and today it is often known as Château Lafite Rothschild.

Even the greatest vineyards have their ups and downs, of course, but the glorious summer of 1787 produced a vintage that was widely acknowledged as one for the ages. However, Bordeaux wines have a drinkable lifespan of no more than 50 years. Today, the contents of this once-glorious 1787 Lafite would, almost certainly, taste about as good as table vinegar. But to find out for certain, you'll need the permission of the Forbes Collection to test it – and it seems unlikely that they would say yes.

Top-end bottles of wine are generally sold at auction, where bidders get caught up in the heat of battle – Forbes clearly won on the day, but there must have been an underbidder willing to bid US$150,000. Unsurprisingly, 1787 Lafites seldom come on to the market. Nonetheless, other bottles of the vintage have since been sold on the internet for less than the 1985 price – though they lack the presidential link. So if you have US$120,000 burning a hole in your pocket, why not treat yourself to a bottle and sprinkle it over your fish and chips?

13 Become a Formula One champion

WHAT IT IS Proving yourself as the world's best driver
WHY YOU WON'T DO IT It's a sport for fearless speed demons only

Formula One (officially known as the FIA Formula One World Championship or simply F1) is the pinnacle of motor racing – a multi-billion-dollar industry with no more than 24 F1 drivers at any one time. Teams spend up to US$200 million dollars a season to compete, so what does it take to become the best of the elite?

Formula One cars are some of the most highly engineered vehicles in the world – only a jet aircraft can come close. With a bullet-shaped one-man cockpit disguised by spoilers that keep it on the tarmac, each car's engine can run at up to 18,000 rpm, enabling it to reach speeds of 350 kilometres per hour (217 mph), and to exert a crushing five times the force of gravity when cornering. Unsurprisingly, then, this isn't a job for your average Sunday motorist – an F1 driver must be physically strong, have remarkable stamina and concentration, quick reflexes, courage and an insatiable hunger to reach the chequered flag first.

Earning a place on an F1 team is a rare achievement. Each team runs only two principal drivers, with contenders often serving as test or reserve drivers before taking one of the main places in a team. For most, the call never comes. The lucky ones can expect salaries of seven and eight figures.

The average age of an F1 driver is in the late twenties, and most started in karting when they could still count their age on the fingers of two hands, then gradually progressed up the less powerful motor-racing classes. However, the need to gain experience of both these powerful machines and the globe-spanning network of F1 circuits means that the leading drivers are usually in their thirties (although in recent times the likes of Lewis Hamilton and Sebastian Vettel have shown that you can make it to world champion in your early twenties)

Being British could offer an advantage – Britain holds the record for both the number of championships won (14) and most individual champion drivers (10). Brazil and Finland, in joint second place, have produced three champions each. And being male certainly gives you an edge – only five women have raced in full competition during more than six decades of F1 history, compared to more than 800 men.

Driving the cars is uncomfortable and intensely physically demanding – for all their complex design features, driver

PIT STOP *British driver Jenson Button takes his McLaren Mercedes F1 car into the pits during testing ahead of the 2010 Spanish Grand Prix, held at the Montmeló track near Barcelona.*

G-forces experienced during cornering, for instance, means that you'll need the strength to keep your head upright when it is some five times heavier than normal. No wonder drivers work hard on general physical fitness, spending an average of 20 hours per week on endurance training and muscle development. Drivers will also maintain a racing heart rate of between 150 and 190 beats per minute for the duration of a race, which can be up to two hours. It all adds up to a phenomenal exertion.

Yet despite the need for physical fitness, drivers acknowledge that the difference between winners and losers is all in the mind. You'll need an ability to retain focus despite all the distractions around you, reacting to rapidly changing circumstances and dealing with high-speed corners, twists and turns while fending off competitors and the inevitable fatigue. For all the safeguards introduced to the sport in recent years, you must also deal with the fact that you run significant risk of death or serious injury every time you go to work.

Each race is preceded by two days of practice and qualification to decide the all-important starting order on the grid. On race day itself, the cars must be in position half an hour before the race start, and no one but the drivers can be on the grid for the final five minutes. During the race, you'll need to observe all safety rules to avoid penalties or even disqualification.

Finally, if you're determined to reach the top, make sure you have room at home for those unfeasibly big trophies.

comfort is not a high priority in Formula One cars. For instance, although the cockpit must meet certain minimum size requirements, each driver's seat is manufactured to precisely fit their body shape, and as a result your range of mobility will be restricted only to the minimum necessary for driving. You don't want to fall victim to an insatiable itch halfway through a race! In addition, you'll be wearing an uncomfortably hot uniform of boots, overalls, gloves and helmet, all made from fire-resistant materials, and a bulky collar designed to protect your head and spinal column in the event of an accident.

As your body is subjected to extreme forces throughout the race, you'll be taking quite a pummelling. The large

14 Tickle yourself

WHAT IT IS
Self-administering
chuckles
WHY YOU WON'T DO IT
Because you'll lack the
element of surprise

You might be one of those people who rolls around uncontrollably and laughs like a drain at the merest hint of someone tickling you. But try to replicate the sensation with nothing more than your own fair hand and the chances are that it's just not going to happen – for some reason, the vast majority of people are simply immune to self-tickling.

'If you tickle us, do we not laugh?' wrote William Shakespeare in *The Merchant of Venice*. But the real trick is to tickle yourself. A few trenchant investigators swear that auto-tickling is possible – they suggest that teasing the soles of your feet with a feather or rotating your tongue in wide arcs around the roof of your mouth can do the trick. Evidence, however, would suggest that plenty of us remain steadfastly immune to the giggles however much we try to provoke ourselves.

The fact is that our laughter when someone else tickles us is fundamentally related to the element of surprise, and the lack of control we have over the situation. Our brains are pretty adept at anticipating sensations so that we ignore what is predictable and safe and focus on what is unexpected and potentially threatening. For instance, brushing your own fingers up your arm is unlikely to cause you to flinch. But if a spider scuttles up your arm, it can send shivers right through you (especially if it turns out to be a tarantula!).

Specifically, when it comes to self-tickling, the part of your brain responsible for motor control (which resides, so far as neuroscientists can work these things out, in a region known as the cerebellum) tells the bit responsible for processing touch (the somatosensory cortex) and the bit responsible for processing 'enjoyable' information (the anterior cingulate cortex) not to get too worked up.

However, help is at hand. A team of scientists from University College, London have designed a remote-controlled (and predictably costly) robot, armed with a probe that has a bit of soft foam mounted at its tip. The 'patient' lies on his or her back with eyes closed, and uses a joystick to control the robot, which attacks them with its ticking stick. A time delay system ensures that when the robot strikes, the crucial element of surprise is retained.

Which is all very impressive – but it's still a lot more fun if you can get someone else to tickle you instead.

15 Swim the Channel

WHAT IT IS Braving the waters between England and France

WHY YOU WON'T DO IT You'll need more than your 25-metre swimming badge to survive the chilly and choppy waters

In 1875 Captain Matthew Webb became the first person to swim the English Channel, in 21 hours 45 minutes. Since then a little over a thousand swimmers have completed the journey. Considerably fewer than half of all solo attempts end in success, and the crossing is still described as 'the Everest of open-water swimming'.

Before even contemplating this arduous challenge, you'll need to be a competent swimmer with good experience of dealing with open water. Getting ready for an attempt is time-consuming and requires total commitment. The Channel is known for its strong tides that change direction every six hours, and its weather is notoriously unpredictable.

The classic (and shortest) route is between Shakespeare Beach, Dover, and Cap Gris Nez on the French side, a distance of 33.6 kilometres (18.2 nautical miles or 20.9 statute miles). Only swims in the direction from England to France are permitted. The Channel is among the world's busiest waterways, with 600 commercial ship movements and 80–100 ferry crossings each day, so you'll rely on a pilot to lead you safely through. They'll also help keep an eye out for hazardous flotsam and jetsam.

In general, there are about 13 days a year when conditions are most suited to crossing attempts. The current record stands at a few minutes under seven hours, but your swim is likely to take between 10 and 20 hours.

Two major bodies can verify crossings: the Channel Swimming Association and the Channel Swimming and Piloting Federation. If you want their recognition, you'll need to follow some rules:
• Swimmers are not allowed to use any artificial aids and can have no physical contact with others during an attempt.
• Swimming costumes should not cover the arms or legs, and should not offer thermal protection or aid buoyancy. Goggles, swimming caps, nose clips and earplugs are permitted.
• Each attempt will be watched by an official observer, who submits a report.
• Your pilot will also be required to hand over positional charts for the swim.

Employ a coach to take you through specialist training. Your regime should certainly include cold-water swimming, since you will probably face temperatures of 13–18°C (55–64.5°F) – hypothermia is among the leading reasons for unsuccessful attempts.

WATER BABY *Zhang Jian, a physical education teacher from the University of Beijing, became the first Chinese man to swim the Channel when he completed a crossing from Dover on the English coast to Calais in France in July 2001.*

Work on developing your bilateral breathing. This will even out your stroke, and allow you to swim on either side of your support vessel – useful for protecting yourself in poor weather.

As well as training in the water, use weights, run, cycle, do circuits and work on your flexibility. Aim to complete a swim of about ten hours three weeks before your crossing, but restrict training to two hours a day in the final fortnight. On the day itself, warm up properly and grease yourself up. This will provide insulation when you enter the water, can protect against mild jellyfish stings and acts as a barrier against chafing. Once the grease is on, ensure it doesn't get on your hands, face or goggles.

You can expect to use up between 600 and 900 calories per hour, so it's a good idea to build up your body fat before an attempt – a little extra padding will also insulate you. Eat regularly during the swim. Many swimmers feed once every hour for the first four hours, then every 30 minutes after that. Aim to keep feeding stops down to a minute or two: you'll need high-energy foods and sports drinks. To avoid human contact, have food delivered via a net or bag attached to a pole or length of string. Expect to swallow large volumes of vomit-inducing salt water despite your best efforts. Like a marathon runner, you are likely to hit 'the wall'. For most swimmers, this comes somewhere between five and eight hours into the swim. Grit your teeth and stick with it.

Don't forget to take out insurance, and be sure to leave your passport with your pilot – after all that effort you don't want to be turned away at the French border!

16 Fly like a bird

WHAT IT IS Your chance to glide like an eagle
WHY YOU WON'T DO IT Unlike a bird, you aren't designed to fly

Since time immemorial, man has wanted to fly. And now we can, in the comfort and relative safety of an aeroplane, helicopter, glider or balloon. Yet still there are some who strive for self-powered flight. Did we learn nothing from the Greek fable of Icarus, who flew too close to the Sun and melted his waxen wings? Apparently not!

Every year at piers around the world, certain doughty individuals don a pair of wings and launch themselves seawards, flapping madly for a moment or two before they plummet into the waves. It is not very effective and hardly dignified.

However, there is a more convincing method of soaring in the air like a bird (or at least a flying squirrel) – the wingsuit. Available for a mere US$600 or so, this is a suit made from durable fabric and worn by daredevils who fling themselves out of aeroplanes. Unlike regular parachutists or skydivers, wingsuit wearers don't immediately enter into free fall but instead 'fly'.

Prototype suits were developed in the 1930s but were hugely unreliable, with several of the early pioneers dying while testing them out. However, in the 1980s Christoph Aarns, a German skydiver, made a great leap forward by augmenting his flying suit with extra webbing. The project was further advanced in the 1990s by Frenchman Patrick de Gayardon, who designed a suit with wing webbing between the legs and under each arm. The wingsuit that we know today was born, and it became commercially available in 1998.

Jumping in a wingsuit has been likened to a cross between skydiving and gliding. It's certainly not a sport for beginners, and before attempting a jump, experts recommend that you complete 500 regular skydives.

Once you jump from your plane, spread your arms and legs to open the wings. The sensations you will feel are quite different to skydiving. Skydivers hurtle groundwards at some 195 kilometres per hour (120 mph) and can surge forward through the air at up to 100 kilometres per hour (62 mph). Wingsuit flyers, in contrast, fall about half as slowly as skydivers, but achieve horizontal speeds up to 145 kilometres per hour (90 mph).

This is because the suit transforms your body into an airfoil, allowing you to generate lots of lift and counter the

SPORT AND LEISURE **49**

MODERN ICARUS *On 27 February 1935, birdman and daredevil Clem Sohn strapped on some wings and webbing of his own invention (weighing about 3.5 kilograms or 8 lb) and jumped from a plane some 3,600 metres (12,000 ft) above Daytona Beach in Florida. He survived to tell the tale. Opposite: modern wingsuits are rather more sophisticated.*

Learn how to adjust your body shape to turn in the air. Keep movements small and controlled to avoid dangerous spins. And no matter how bird-like you feel, don't be tempted to flap your arms, as this could result in you going into a disastrous dive or spin.

Once you're feeling confident and have honed your flying skills, throw some mid-air acrobatics into your display. But don't get too carried away, and remember, as your inevitable descent picks up speed, you will eventually need to deploy your parachute!

As something to aim for, in 2012 Japanese wingsuit flyer Shinichi Ito flew for a record horizontal distance of 26.9 kilometres (16.7 miles) above Yolo County, Califonia, remaining airborne for more than five minutes.

effects of gravity in just the same way as an aircraft wing. The extra lift helps improve your glide ratio (the relationship between gravity, lift and drag) making it possible for you to advance forwards through the air.

Flying requires careful management of your rate of fall to create the optimum balance of lift and drag. Roll your shoulders forwards and tuck your chin into your neck to maximize forward propulsion. To increase your flying time (but reduce propulsion), lift your head and look forwards, bend at the hips, extend your arms and legs and 'push down' against the upward force.

Of course, if the harnessed power of gravity isn't enough for you, there's always the wingpack. This development of the wingsuit consists of strap-on carbon-fibre wings with a small integrated jet engine. While the technology is still in its infancy, it has had marked successes – in 2003 Austrian daredevil Felix Baumgartner (see page 210) used a wingpack to cross the English Channel.

But still, there is a way to go before we truly rival the birds. Consider for instance the humble pigeon, who can cover a distance 75 times its own body length in a single second!

Become a billionaire

17

WHAT IT IS The amassing of almost unimaginable wealth
WHY YOU WON'T DO IT That much money never comes easily

'Who wants to be a millionaire?' asked the old song. Not us, comes the reply – these days we want to be billionaires. We want to live the life of the super-rich in our plush mansions and aboard our private yachts. And of course we want to save the world with our charitable foundations. So how can we make a start?

As of 2011, *Forbes Magazine* – the rich man's guide to everything – documented 1,210 US dollar billionaires throughout the world, with a total net worth of US$4.5 trillion. You have the best chance of finding yourself among their ranks if you are American – the US boasts 413, Asia 332, Europe 300 and the rest of the world 165. The average age of a billionaire in the *Forbes* survey was 66.

A few of these super-rich individuals are born into their money. The King of Saudi Arabia, for instance, has an estimated net worth of US$21 billion and Albert II of Monaco can boast a cool US$1 billion. Queen Elizabeth II of England, perhaps surprisingly, falls below the billion-dollar threshold.

However, the majority of billionaires make their own fortune, and the list of industries in which they have made their megabucks is a surprisingly long and varied one (although you can probably rule out certain professions such as teacher or charity worker).

According to *Forbes*, the world's seven richest people in 2013 were Carlos Slim of Mexico, Bill Gates, Warren Buffett, Larry Ellison and Charles and David Koch (all from the USA), and Amancio Ortega of Spain. Slim made his fortune primarily from telecommunications, Gates and Ellison from IT, Buffett from investments, the Koch brothers from oil and chemicals, and Ortega from fashion.

There are few hard and fast rules about how to become a billionaire, but many of the super-rich seem to share certain characteristics. Researching the lives of the rich to understand what motivates them, why they behave in particular ways and what attitudes they have, will give you a better chance of joining them.

In the first place, they really are only human. Despite their wealth, they go through many of the same ups and downs as the rest of us. They worry about their health, about their relationships, about whether their child is going to pass their spelling

TOP TRUMP *Donald Trump is one of America's most famous business magnates and media personalities, with a net worth estimated at over US$3 billion, some of which he used to build the iconic Trump Tower in Manhattan. And all that wealth brings other privileges – Trump is now part of the entertainment elite, famous for his appearances on reality television show* **The Apprentice,** *and able to hobnob with the likes of Miss Universe 2012, Olivia Culpo.*

problem-solve in creative ways and have highly developed analytical faculties that allow them to strike straight to the heart of a problem. This also helps them to identify commercial opportunities.

They also tend to have started their careers with clear, staged goals in mind, not the least of which is to make lots of money – there are not many accidental billionaires.

As such, the self-made super-rich tend to be risk-takers who are unafraid to fail. A great many billionaires have made and lost their fortunes at least once, but they demonstrate the ability to bounce back stronger, using previous failures as learning experiences.

Many claim billionaires have a strong understanding of human psychology, enabling them to persuade people to share in their vision, make sacrifices on their behalf and, ultimately, help them get rich. Poverty (or at least, relative poverty) in early life is a recurrent trait, presumably providing the motivation not to return to that state. A secure and supportive family background in the early stages of wealth accumulation is another often-mentioned factor.

Finally, in interviews billionaires seem keen to emphasize that money is not everything after all. But then they would say that, wouldn't they?

test on Monday. They might not have to worry about paying the mortgage, but they are at the top of such finely poised financial empires that even they sometimes experience cash-flow issues. In short, they are not so different to you or me. However, studies suggest that billionaires display the ability to

20 Break a world record

WHAT IT IS Doing something that no one has ever done before **WHY YOU WON'T DO IT** If it *was* easy, someone would have already done it

For many, *Guiness World Records* is the record-breakers Bible. Most record-breakers aspire to see their name within its hallowed pages. So do you think you could smash more than 70 watermelons in a minute by punching them? Or pass yourself through a tennis racket over seven times in three minutes? If so you could join that exclusive club.

Before undertaking any record attempt, check that the record is an accepted one. Many are not, often on safety grounds (for instance, certain extreme eating and drinking records have been phased out in recent years). About a quarter of records in the book are broken each year, and there are 65,000 applications for inclusion processed. You'll need to provide evidence of any record claim, including two unbiased witness testimonies and a logbook. In general, record attempts should be made in a public place. Verification is often aided by the presence of local media too. You will normally receive a response to indicate whether your claim has been validated within six weeks.

You have more chance of getting into print if you challenge an established record – you *can* suggest a new category but be sure to get approval from the book's editorial team so that you don't waste time setting a record that they won't accept. Records must be challenging, provable, quantifiable and breakable. They should not be specific to the individual. You can also check with the editorial team for the current record standard, which might have changed since the latest edition of the book was published.

Be realistic in the records you aim for. Are you really going to beat Usain Bolt over 100 metres? Are you physically capable of outgrowing the 27 centimetres (11 in) needed to claim the longest beard on a living woman? Play to your strengths – perhaps amassing the world's largest ball of string is rather more up your street? This is how New Yorker Ashrita Furman got to hold more records than anyone else, currently 151 entries in the book, and more than 400 set since he started collecting them in 1979. Furman counts jumping jacks, yodelling, pogo sticking up Mount Fuji, juggling underwater (shown opposite), playing hopscotch and walking with a bottle of milk on his head among his achievements. And needless to say, he also holds the record for 'Most Guiness World Records held by an individual at the same time.'

21 Break the bank at Monte Carlo

WHAT IT IS Beating the odds to defeat the House
WHY YOU WON'T DO IT Gambling is a mug's game

It is a simple truth that you never meet a poor casino owner and rarely meet a wealthy gambler. And aside from Las Vegas, there is nowhere in the world quite so known for gambling as Monte Carlo in Monaco, with its beautiful casino basking in the Mediterranean sun. So what are your best options for making the croupiers weep?

The original 'man who broke the bank at Monte Carlo' was one Joseph Jagger, a Briton who in the 1870s made hay after spotting a roulette wheel with a bias towards certain numbers. If you hope to follow in Jagger's footsteps, you can generally start gambling from 2 p.m., but there are certain rules of admission, principally that you must be over 18 years of age and should dress smartly. There's a modest admission charge, and various games on offer.

As with any form of gambling you should never bet more than you are prepared to lose – it's easy to get caught up in the moment, but you may regret it in the morning. The rules for roulette are simple: you bet on a number or set of numbers (from 1 to 36) and if a spun ball lands in the corresponding slot of the roulette wheel, you win. If you bet on a single number, the odds are obviously 35-1. Other types of bet offer odds on a gradually reducing scale. Simple enough? In fact, roulette is widely regarded as one of the most difficult games to win – not least because the wheel includes a zero slot that tips the odds in the house's favour by more than 5 per cent!

Most experts believe that you have a better chance of beating the house at the blackjack table. In this game, you're initially dealt two cards, and your aim is to get a total as close to 21 as possible without exceeding it ('going bust'). You then have to decide whether to risk adding cards to the hand and increase its value – you win if your hand beats the dealer's without going bust, or if the dealer himself exceeds 21. There are various clever rules of thumb for working out if the odds favour you 'hitting' (adding another card) or 'standing' in various scenarios, and if you can remember them all, they may tip the odds slightly in your favour.

Of course, if you've got the nerve for it, there is also card counting, a test of memory and mental arithmetic that involves keeping track of the dealing in any card game to work out whether a high or low card is likely to be dealt next.

22 Write a hit record

WHAT IT IS Penning a
chart-topping tune
WHY YOU WON'T DO IT
Besides talent, you need
big luck and bigger bucks

Despite the changing landscape of the music industry, there is still nothing quite like having a Number One record to your name. It might be tricky to keep track of the many different charts – physical sales, air play, digital downloads and so on – but in the end it's all about having a song that people want to listen to.

Writing songs is a bit like kissing frogs in search of a prince. You'll probably have to write a lot of them before you hit upon the one. For instance, Guy Chambers, Robbie Williams's former writing partner and one of today's most successful hitmakers, reportedly scores one hit for every 47 songs he writes. And songs don't write themselves, so get on with it – a bit of daydreaming is fine, but you need to get all those words and tunes that are in your head down on paper.

Having a Number One hit is a delicate balance of quality songwriting, great performance, clever marketing and great good luck. Immerse yourself in music. Seek out different styles from different eras. Educate yourself in the theory of songwriting – you don't have to spend years at a salon, but it helps to have a basic understanding of melody, harmony and rhythm. Familiarize yourself with basic song structures. Don't be constricted by theory, but use it to free your creativity. According to *Billboard Magazine*, the average length of a hit song is 4.26 minutes, with a tempo between 117 and 122 beats per minute. For your best statistical chance of a hit, write in the key of C and stick to major keys. If you struggle with lyrics, get a partner to look after that side of things – an arrangement that worked out nicely for Elton John and Bernie Taupin.

When you have a song that you think might work, play it to people. If they don't leave whistling it, perhaps it's not your hit. However, be sure to copyright your song and don't sell the rights too cheaply or without royalties. Decide if you want to link up with a major record label or not. A multinational will always have the resources and know-how to reach places that you as an individual might not, but increasingly musicians are able to strike out on their own or on smaller labels. Once upon a time, a record's success depended on radio airplay – if the DJs were on your side, the chances of your song succeeding were good. These days, thanks to the internet, there are more methods than ever of garnering attention, and a wily songwriter will make use of all of them.

23 Be modelled by Madame Tussauds

WHAT IT IS Securing
immortality in wax
WHY YOU WON'T DO IT
Fame is fickle and can
come and go in the time
it take to get modelled

There is fame, and then there is being immortalized in wax at the famous Madame Tussauds in London. The modelling process is a time-consuming one that demands that your fame lasts rather more than the proverbial 15 minutes, but once you're on display, you can expect to feature in countless holiday snaps with bedazzled tourists.

Madame Tussaud was born Anna Maria Grosholtz in Strasbourg in 1761 and established her first London museum in Marylebone in the early years of the 19th century. Over the ensuing centuries, its methods of model-making have changed dramatically.

If you want to earn your place in front of the hordes of tourists, your first move should be to become a household name. The London museum introduces 10–12 new models per year, and each can take up to six months to perfect. As a result, Madame Tussauds is not bothered about fly-by-nights or the stars of the underground. If you're the Queen, great! Barack Obama, yes! Lady Gaga, come in! In the fame stakes, aim high.

Having received the call that you're to be featured, you'll be working with Merlin Studios of Acton in West London on your casting. The first step is to arrange your visit to the studios. Sittings can be as short as 15 minutes, but about four hours is more desirable. You'll meet with the sculptor, their assistant, specialists

in hair, eyes, skin and wardrobe, and a team to mould your teeth and hands. You'll discuss the general image of the model, including expression and pose. The sculptor will take copious photographs and precise measurements, but they will also try to get to know the 'real you', in the hope that the model captures the essence of your personality.

The sculptor then spends several weeks sculpting in clay. Along with the photos taken at the sitting, they will use press photos and video footage for inspiration. An armature (that's your skeleton) is built up out of steel and aluminium rods, newspaper padding and chicken wire – you might be famous but it's not all glamour.

Once the neck has been perfected, your head will be removed for detailed work. Incidentally, your sculpted head will be made larger than it really is in order to make up for shrinkage during the wax casting process. The whole sculpting process can take anything from 10 to 12 weeks.

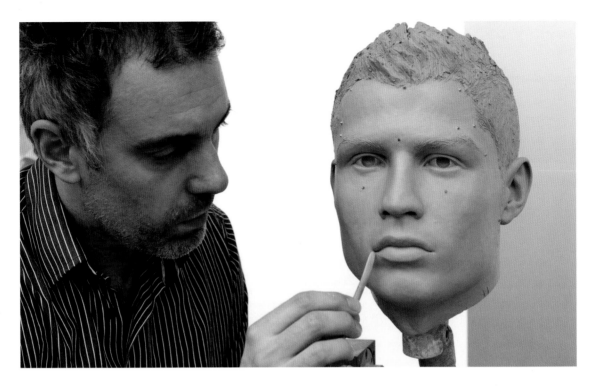

KEY PLAYER *A Tussauds sculptor puts the finishing touches to a clay bust of Portuguese football superstar Cristiano Ronaldo, prior to casting in wax. Ronaldo made his debut in time to celebrate the FIFA World Cup in a 'fantasy football' team that also included England's David Beckham and Brazil's legendary Pelé.*

Next comes the moulding and casting stage. The head and hands (the bits most on display, unless you're Lady Gaga) are treated separately from the rest of the body. A beeswax and Japan wax mix is used to cast the head, and the plaster moulds are built to last up to 200 years in case repairs are needed in the future. Your head is cast in many sections, then returned to the sculptor after assembly for 'ironing out' of any joins.

Your hands will be cast in dental alginate, a strong and flexible material that reproduces all the lines, pores and hair follicles in your skin. Your body, meanwhile, will be cast in resin and fibreglass. Oil paints are used to detail your head and hands – the head typically takes five days, with a further two days for the hands. The eyes are painted with watercolours, their colours sourced to perfectly match your real eyes. Making them takes ten hours, while a full set of gnashers can take a teeth-grinding four days. Using impressions taken at your sitting, they are made with materials bought from dental suppliers. Each tooth is then individually coloured and polished. Meanwhile, a hair merchant matches hair to a sample taken at your sitting. Each strand is individually inserted with special tools in a marathon six-week 'thatching'.

Finally, you'll be clothed – normally the museum asks you to donate some of your own clothes but if this is not possible, exact copies can be sourced from the appropriate shop or tailor. So there you go – but if you do get the call from Tussaud's, just make sure they are not planning to put you into the Chamber of Horrors!

24 Steal the Mona Lisa

WHAT IT IS Pilfering the world's best-known portrait
WHY YOU WON'T DO IT There is no better protected 'enigmatic smile' in the world

The most famous artwork in the world, the *Mona Lisa* by Leonardo da Vinci takes pride of place in the Louvre in Paris. The portrait of Lisa, wife of Francesco del Giocondo (hence the work's alternative name *La Gioconda*) was considered unfinished by the artist at the time of his death in 1519. Seen by some 8 million people per year, it is among the world's best-guarded treasures.

As one of the world's leading museums, the converted French royal palace of the Louvre today combines the strength of a medieval castle with the latest in high-tech security, making it a fitting home for many of the greatest art treasures in the world. More than a thousand guards patrol the building around the clock, and 8.9 million tourists amble through its maze-like complex of galleries every year (an average of almost 29,000 each day), and most of them make a beeline for the enormous hall known as the Salle des États.

Here, in incongruously modernist surroundings (the Salle was refurbished in 2005), the *Mona Lisa* sits in a custom-built, climate-controlled, sealed frame, smiling her enigmatic smile from behind 5-centimetre-thick (2-in) bulletproof glass. A table-like platform built into the wall beneath her stops visitors from getting within 2.4 metres (8 ft) ,

SAFE RETURN *Italian and French officials celebrate* La Gioconda's *return to her home in the Louvre in December 1913, following her theft more than two years previously. The disappearance of the* Mona Lisa *and her later restoration played a key role in turning the painting into the international icon it remains to this day.*

cameras keep her under constant video surveillance and motion sensors ensure no unauthorized person thinks about getting too close. All in all, your chances of grabbing some 'alone time' with the most famous woman in the world are close to zero.

It wasn't always this way, however. A century ago, *La Gioconda* hadn't quite become the global icon she is today, and her surroundings were a lot more low-key. As a result, one man did famously succeed in stealing the masterpiece.

The name of this daredevil was Vincenzo Peruggia, an amateur artist born near Milan. Despite spending several years living in Paris, he remained a firm Italian nationalist and laboured under the misapprehension that the *Mona Lisa* had been looted from Italy by Napoleon.

While the Louvre did (and still does) contain many works obtained like this, the *Mona Lisa* was not one of them – she was bought entirely legally by the French King Francis I (a significant patron of Da Vinci) shortly after the artist's death.

Obsessed with the idea of returning *Mona Lisa* to her homeland, Peruggia spent several months in 1911 working as a handyman at the Louvre, becoming familiar with the layout of the museum and the habits of its employees.

On Sunday, 20 August 1911 he put his plan into action. Wearing his museum uniform so that he could move around unchallenged, he concealed himself in a storeroom overnight, only to emerge on Monday morning (at the time, the museum's traditional closure day). Mingling with the maintenance crews,

Peruggia then made his way to the *Mona Lisa*, lifted her from the wall in the Salon Carré and made his way to the relative privacy of a stairwell – all without encountering a single guard. Cutting the painting from its cumbersome frame, he wrapped *La Gioconda* in a sheet, tucked her under his arm and made for the exit – only to find he was locked in. Just as Peruggia must have thought that the game was up, a plumber appeared and seeing a colleague in official uniform (but not noticing the frame now propped up against the wall), used his set of keys to liberate the thief. The *Mona Lisa*'s disappearing act was not discovered until the Louvre reopened to the public on the Tuesday morning.

Vincenzo Peruggia took the picture to his apartment, where he kept it for two years without attracting suspicion. He then smuggled the *Mona Lisa* to Florence, and contacted art dealer Alfredo Geri, claiming he wanted to return her to her rightful home. However, Geri called in an expert from the Uffizi Gallery to confirm its authenticity, and Peruggia served seven months in prison, though he also became something of a national hero in some quarters. *Mona Lisa*, meanwhile, was returned to Paris after a brief tour of Italy.

Needless to say, if you try to emulate Peruggia today, you'll be up against a lot more security – and it might be worth bearing in mind that the museum's weekly closures are now on Tuesdays!

SPLENDID ISOLATION *Since 2005, the* Mona Lisa *has been displayed on a wall of her own in the Louvre's Salle des États, surrounded by security features to keep her admirers at a safe distance.*

Own a Shakespeare First Folio

WHAT IT IS The original collection of the Bard's great works
WHY YOU WON'T DO IT Its rarity is reflected in its astronomical value

Browsing an antiquarian bookshop offers many puzzles for the avid bibliophile. Is a book collectible? Is it a first edition? Signed? In good condition? But you don't need to be an expert to know that if you come into possession of a Shakespeare First Folio, you're onto a good thing.

When William Shakespeare shuffled off his mortal coil in 1616, he left an unrivalled body of literature, but it was to be a further seven years before all of his plays were collected together in one volume. Compiled by his friends John Hemminge and Henry Condell, each edition in the print run of a mere 750 was unique, boasting its own array of typographical errors and printer's corrections. It sold for £1, equivalent to US$200 in modern money. These days experts believe that around 230 copies survive, mostly owned by major institutions – the Folger Shakespeare Library in Washington, D.C., for example, accounts for 82 copies alone.

But what if you want one in your own study? Your best option is to be very rich. You'll definitely need more than that original £1 – or even the inflation-adjusted US$200. You will also need some patience – First Folios pop up only rarely at the auction house, and when one does, super-rich collectors fight it out with museums and libraries. A copy sold in July 2006 fetched US$5.2 million.

If that seems beyond your reach, then why not rely on simple good fortune? Take the example of Anne Humphries, a Manchester housewife whose life was turned upside down in 2004 when she inherited a book from a long-lost relative. The volume, long assumed to be a convincing facsimile, was revealed under expert inspection as a genuine First Folio. The North of England seems to be a good place to locate yourself if you're taking the 'lucky break' route: a few years later another long-forgotten copy turned up in a council storeroom at Skipton Public Library in Yorkshire.

One method we cannot recommend is theft. A copy that turned up at the Folger Library in 2008 was soon identified as the mutilated remains of a copy stolen from Durham University a decade before. It had been brought to the Folger by one Raymond Scott, who lived not far from Durham but claimed to have stumbled across the volume in Cuba. Acquitted of theft, he was nevertheless convicted of handling stolen goods and received an eight-year sentence for his trouble.

26 Win an Oscar™

WHAT IT IS Making it to the top of the Hollywood tree
WHY YOU WON'T DO IT Once in a lifetime roles are hard to come by

There are 24 categories of Academy Award to choose from, but we're not interested in make-up or sound mixing here. We're talking the big five: best picture, director, actor, actress and screenplay. In fact, scratch that last one – famously in the movie business, no one cares about the writer!

If you're serious about getting hold of that famous golden statuette, you'll need to plan your project carefully from the outset. In the best picture competition, horror is out, as are sci-fi, comedy and musicals (with the notable recent exception of *Chicago*). Fantasy is another no-no, unless you're Peter Jackson: as a rule, keep it gritty and realistic. The Academy also favours length – no winner has been less than 90 minutes, while *Gone with the Wind*, *Ben Hur* and *Lawrence of Arabia* all ran for more than 210 minutes.

If you're aiming for best director, don't be a woman – the only female winner so far is Kathryn Bigelow for *The Hurt Locker* in 2009. Statistically, you stand most chance as a straight, white man. There has only ever been one winner of Asian origin (Ang Lee, though he's won twice), and four out gay or bisexual winners. Only two black directors have ever been nominated.

Best actresses are, on average, aged 35, but there is hope if you're older: Jessica Tandy was 80 when she won in 1989. If you're naturally beautiful, try playing ugly – think Charlize Theron in *Monster* or Nicole Kidman in *The Hours*. It's also smart to play a real person – 70 per cent of recent winners have done this. Best actors are older, averaging 43. Again, playing someone real is a smart move. Historically, mental disorders, addictions and disabilities are also fruitful subjects. Speak English, unless you're Roberto Benigni in *Life is Beautiful* (though French actor Jean Dujardin won in 2012 for a silent performance in *The Artist*).

Your Oscar campaign will need studio backing to the tune of US$2–3 million. Sony spent US$5 million on *The Social Network* in 2011, and still lost out on best picture. The ceremony itself is watched by a billion people around the world, and is the showcase of the movie industry – so if you're summoned to the red carpet, be prepared to splash even more cash on styling, clothes and jewellery. You have 45 seconds for your acceptance speech before they play you off – don't waste it, and don't forget to thank your mum.

Make it on Broadway

27

WHAT IT IS Becoming
the biggest star in
Theatre-Land
WHY YOU WON'T DO IT
There is always someone
younger, hungrier and
more talented...

Have you ever wanted to see your name in lights on Broadway?
Conquering New York's famous theatre district is the ultimate
ambition for many in the world of entertainment. After all, as Ol' Blue
Eyes himself so memorably noted, 'If I can make it there, I'll make
it anywhere.'

Every year, thousands of starry-eyed
hopefuls flock to New York in the hope
of making it big in showbusiness, but
for most of them, the dream remains
just that. If you want to avoid the pitfalls
and make it big, you'll need to hone
your skills. Start out acting in amateur
productions, take as many courses as
you can and go to drama school. Read up
on the great acting theorists – the likes
of Stanislavski, Meisner and Grotowski.
Look after yourself physically – your body
is your tool so treat it with respect.

Try to be a triple threat – if you can sing
and dance as well as act you'll massively
increase your chances of landing that
big break. Take vocal lessons even if you
don't plan to focus on singing, as you will
also develop greater control over your
speaking voice. Similarly, dance classes
can improve your general movement and
fitness even if you're no Gene Kelly.

Arrive in the Big Apple with a plan – do
your homework before arriving and, once
there, familiarize yourself with the scene
quickly. Who do you need to meet? Where

do you go to get an audition? Make sure
you have a résumé and headshots, and
thrust them in the general direction of
anyone who might be able to help you.
Your chances of success are also hugely
increased if you're a member of the
Equity union. Without that famous Equity
card, you'll be left struggling to stand
out from the crowd at rare open call
auditions. Many actors work regionally
before going to New York, as it can be
easier to earn your card that way.

When you go for an audition, try to make
the role your own. Opt for an interesting
audition piece that showcases your skills
and individuality – if you're the hundredth
person that day delivering 'To be or not
to be...', the producers will probably
answer 'not to be'. If you're required to
perform a song, the Broadway standard
is to have 32 bars of music prepared. If
you have to dance, remember to pack
your dancing shoes. And don't waste
time going for roles that aren't right for
you. If you're a six-foot-three, tatooed,
African-American male, don't waste your
time going for the lead in *Annie*.

Sing the lead at La Scala

WHAT IT IS Holding court at the world's most famous opera venue
WHY YOU WON'T DO IT Only a chosen few have the lungs for it

As American humourist Ed Gardner once noted: 'Opera is when a guy gets stabbed in the back and, instead of bleeding, he sings.' However, there is much more to being a lead opera singer – whether you're a diva soprano or a brow-mopping tenor – than just the ability to hold a tune, a propensity to plumpness, and a tendency to over-emote.

Perhaps the most famous opera house of them all is La Scala in Milan. Since it opened on 3 August 1778 with a debut performance of *Europa Riconosciuta* by Mozart's rival Antonio Salieri, an appearance at this 3,000-seater venue has represented the pinnacle of many an artist's career. The roll call of great names who have appeared here includes Dame Nellie Melba, Enrico Caruso, Maria Callas, Luciano Pavarotti and Dame Kiri Te Kanawa. So how might you join this grand pantheon?

While the history of pop music is littered with 'overnight stars', they simply don't exist in the opera world. To get to the top is a long road that needs to start early in life. Needless to say, in the first instance you must have the raw talent. If you struggle to hit the high notes in your school choir, then you're unlikely to suddenly develop into a great opera singer in later life.

If, though, you have a rough diamond of a voice, then the long process of polishing it can begin. While some performers specialize in music only once they enter tertiary education, many of the greats spent their childhoods honing their craft in conservatoires. Your vocal technique should allow you to generate a beautiful, even sound across the high, middle and bottom ranges while performing operas that last as long as four hours. You must also be powerful enough to be heard above the roar of a full orchestra.

However, training the voice is but one aspect of an opera singer's training. You will also study musical theory, music history, learn how to sight-read and master the full range of acting skills. You'll need the memory skills to retain large chunks of a libretto too. Oh, and a good working knowledge of French, German, Italian and Russian will stand you in good stead – it's always nice to understand what you're singing. From there, it's simply a case of waiting for the crowds to greet your performance with calls of 'Encore!' Achieving your dream may take perseverance, but as the famous saying goes, it ain't over till the fat lady sings.

29 Have as many lovers as Casanova

WHAT IT IS Being the ultimate chick- or man-magnet
WHY YOU WON'T DO IT Are you really as attractive as all that?

Born in Venice in 1725, Giacomo Girolamo Casanova was one of the great lovers in history, with the notches on his bedpost conservatively estimated at 122. Today his name is synonymous with any man considered to be both promiscuous and unscrupulous – so how might you follow in his somewhat dubious footsteps?

Casanova certainly lived a varied life, with stints as a scholar, lawyer, priest, librarian, soldier, gambler, musician and spy, not to mention a spell in prison. But undoubtedly his greatest work came in the field of seduction. For the great lover, pleasure comes before everything. 'Cultivating whatever gave pleasure to my senses was always the chief business of my life,' as he put it. In short, seduction is not a pastime, it's a job! As such, you should be ready for action whenever the opportunity arises. 'The lover who is not ready to take Fortune by the forelock is lost.'

Casanova never underestimated the power of charm, and believed it was impossible to praise a woman too highly. Being a suave Venetian probably helped, but he also knew how to make a lady laugh. He developed a masterly sense of who might fall for his charm, specializing in women in unhappy relationships. As a general rule, he liked to tell an intelligent woman how beautiful she was, and a beautiful woman how smart she was.

He went to great efforts to set the right mood, hiring expensive hotel rooms, which he filled with candlelight and sweet perfumes. He would also throw lavish feasts, plying his lady friends with rum or champagne punches and feeding them copious amounts of oysters and chocolate (both reputed to have aphrodisiac qualities).

Casanova was prepared to spread his net wide: he spent much of his colourful life pinballing between Venice, Naples, Constantinople, Paris, Amsterdam, London and St Petersburg, with at least one girl in every port. Nor was any type of woman considered off-bounds – his roll call of lovers included servant girls, actresses and nuns. Frankly, he was prepared to give anyone a go!

If you aspire to equal or surpass his rather vulgar number of lovers, remember that we live in an age where safe sex is valued rather more highly than it was in Casanova's day. It's also worth noting that the great lover ended up old, single and sporadically suicidal.

30 Start your own religion

WHAT IT IS The creation of an entire belief system
WHY YOU WON'T DO IT Even if you believe, will anyone else?

Few authorities, it seems, can agree on how many religions, operate in the world. Statistics reveal some 20 major world religions with more than half a million adherents each, but other estimates suggest that there are at least 4,000 different religions currently being practised. Well over a century and a half after Karl Marx proclaimed religion 'the opium of the people', the hunger for faith remains strong.

Around 60 per cent of the world's population claim to have some sort of religious belief, and there's certainly no shortage of options available for the choosy wannabe-believer. But what if you are unable to find a religion that you feel reflects your own belief system? One option is to just found a religion of your own. There is no handbook to tell you how to go about it, but here are a few basic guidelines to bear in mind.

Any religion needs a defined system of belief, usually striving to explain the order of things, our place within that order, and our relationship with one or more deities. Creating your belief system is not something that should be rushed. Many of the most notably successful religions established in more recent times were founded by individuals claiming to have had a spiritual visitation outlining their mission. Consider Joseph Smith, founder of the Church of Jesus Christ of Latter-Day Saints (the Mormons), who said he was visited by Christ himself in 1820. Or Sun Myung Moon of the Moonies, who claimed Jesus visited *him* when he was a 16-year old in 1936 and urged him to proclaim himself the new messiah (one of the group's famous weddings is shown opposite). Another spiritual leader, Guy Ballard, insisted that he had been inspired by the reincarnation of the Comte de Saint Germain, a French occultist who lived in the 18th century, in 1930s California.

Having worked out your faith, you will need to find some believers. In the first instance, you should make sure that your religion at some level has an appeal to others. Promising eternal salvation is generally a winner, but simply trying to make sense of an often confusing world is also a good place to start. Plugging into a sense of disaffection with the world at large may also work. Make your sacred text widely available. From the Talmud, Bible or Quran to the Book of Mormon or L. Ron Hubbard's founding texts of Scientology, getting the word out is vital to a religion's success. Also, while it's often said that the devil has all the best tunes, a few rousing anthems will do your religion no harm at all.

80   FAME, WEALTH AND POWER

FOUNDING FATHER *Left: L. Ron Hubbard, pictured here at his writing desk, was a science fiction author who founded the Church of Scientology in the 1950s. He died in 1986 at the age of 74, but Scientology has gone from strength to strength without him. Today, it boasts a worldwide membership including several figures from Hollywood's glitterati.*

FRUM HERE TO ETERNITY *Opposite: Inside the John Frum sacred hut on Tanna Island in the South Pacific, where one-fifth of the population follow the movement's teachings. Frum, often depicted as a US serviceman, was said to have appeared to islanders in the 1930s. Widely regarded as a 'cargo cult', followers expect ancestral spirits to bestow modern conveniences on the community.*

Consider the location of your base carefully, since some environments are more fertile than others. The United States, for instance, is traditionally highly receptive to religion. Over 40 per cent of the population profess to regularly attend religious services, just under three times as many as in France, four times the figures for the UK and almost six times the rate in Australia. In contrast, Belarus seems a rather less friendly place to set up a new religion – in 2002 a law was passed stating that all religions not registered before 1982 would henceforth be prohibited from recognition as a 'religious association'.

As leader of a religion, you may wish to develop a cult of personality. However, be careful not to believe all your own hype. David Koresh's rise to head the Branch Davidians culminated in his belief that he was the faith's final prophet. Amid accusations of illegal activities, the sect's base in Waco, Texas, was besieged by the FBI in 1993 for more than 50 days, ending in a fire that left more than 80 of

Koresh's believers, including the self-proclaimed Messiah himself, dead.

Official acknowledgement is always a bonus, and can offer legal and monetary advantages. In the UK's 2001 census, 400,000 people said they practised the Jedi faith. Two believers, John Wilkinson and Charlotte Law, subsequently petitioned the UN for the Jedi faith to be recognized as a formal religion. They were unsuccessful, however, since the UN argued that it wasn't in the business of certifying religions.

Many religions posit a Day of Judgement scenario, when we will all be required to account for our actions at the world's end. Just be careful not to predict this event too early. Plenty have made that mistake – most famously in recent times, Californian evangelical preacher Harold Camping has earned himself something of a reputation for miscalled Judgement Days. And after leading your believers to a hilltop to await the end, it can be a long walk back home if it doesn't arrive.

31 Establish your own nation

WHAT IT IS A declaration of sovereignty
WHY YOU WON'T DO IT Any territory worth claiming has already been taken

What makes a country a country? It's a question that's more vexed than you might imagine. Two-thirds of countries, for instance, observe the sovereignty of Palestine, yet it is not recognized by many others. So if you want to set up a state of your own, what's the best way of getting people to accept your little corner of the world as a sovereign nation in its own right?

Eccentric musical genius Frank Zappa claimed the qualifications for statehood were simple: 'You can't be a real country unless you have a beer and an airline – it helps if you have some kind of football team, or some nuclear weapons, but at the very least you need a beer.' Zappa, however, famously called his daughter Moon Unit, so he may not be the most reliable font of wisdom. A more reliable source of information might be the 1933 Montevideo Convention on the Rights and Duties of States. Though the Convention does not have the force of international law, it does represent a widely held set of standards. To be a state, you need at the very least: (a) a permanent population; (b) a defined territory; (c) a government; and (d) capacity to enter into relations with other states.

Assuming you're not keen on staging an invasion of someone else's country and lack the finances to buy one, there are a couple of options when it comes to territory. The simplest is to declare your own property independent, but the chances are that no one will take you very seriously since your land still falls in another nation's territory. Alternatively, look to international waters – if you can find an unclaimed island 22 kilometres (12 nautical miles) beyond any nation's territorial limit and 370 kilometres (200 nautical miles) from any major economic zones, you could be in business.

As head of state, you'll probably want to create a constitution, along with a flag, national anthem and currency. Award yourself a decent title too – North Korean dictator Kim Jong-il enjoyed monikers such as 'Highest Incarnation of the Revolutionary Comradely Love', 'Great Sun of The Nation' and the short but elegant 'Brilliant Leader'. Jean-Bédel Bokassa (opposite) reigned as self-proclaimed Emperor of Central Africa from 1976 to 1979. Finally, how about joining the United Nations? Application requires a standard letter, and to qualify as a member you'll have to promise to uphold UN principles. Unfortunately, you'll also need backing from the General Assembly and Security Council – that's where things could get difficult.

ANYONE FOR TEE?

Above: Northern Irish golfer Rory McIlroy tees off at Amen Corner during the 2012 US Masters. One of the most challenging stretches of the course, the corner encompasses all or part of the fiendishly difficult 11th, 12th and 13th holes. Many a contest has been won and lost there. Right: A map of the legendary Augusta course shows the individual holes along with their par scores.

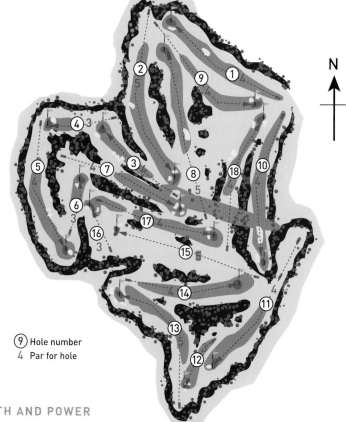

⑨ Hole number
4 Par for hole

you just need to be one of the world's top 90 players (based on current rankings and past tournament success). All in all, if you're serious about this option you should probably be out practising your swing rather than reading this book. And even winning the Masters only gets you limited perks – just one guest per year on the Sunday before the competition.

Alternatively, you could work for the club – employees are entitled to play the course once a year, but competition for jobs is predictably fierce. An outside company recruits caddies for the club – the application process is tough but caddies do get certain playing rights. At the Masters itself, competitors may bring their personal caddies, who can be either male or female. This is one of the only ways for a woman to get onto the course unless invited by a member. The club also employs some 400 volunteers who get the opportunity to play the

course each May. Alas, the waiting list is massive, and rumour has it that it's been closed completely.

You could also become a journalist or broadcaster in the world of golf – after the Masters, there is a draw among the media folk and a lucky 32 get to play a round.

If all else fails, you could always try joining the nearby (and moderately less exclusive) Augusta Country Club. It has been known for members of Augusta National to pop round in search of a player in the event of a last-minute drop-out, so maybe you'll find yourself in the right place at the right time.

And remember, if you do get a chance to play on the hallowed ground, be sure not to be overheard uttering that immortal quotation from Mark Twain about golf being 'a good walk spoiled'.

Bullfight

WHAT IT IS Outwitting a fearsome bovine opponent
WHY YOU WON'T DO IT Who wants to put themselves in the path of a half a tonne of aggression and horns?

Ernest Hemingway once described bullfighting as 'the only art in which the artist is in danger of death and in which the degree of brilliance in the performance is left to the fighter's honour'. While it may never shed its reputation for cruelty, its supporters argue it is a sport of artistry and integrity.

The oldest bullfighting arena still in existence can be found in Seville and dates to around 1765. The largest are to be found in Mexico and can accommodate crowds of up to 50,000. For many, such a sport is simply anachronistic, but there are still plenty of impassioned fans. And whatever your opinion on the ethics, there's certainly more to it than simply waving a red rag at a bull. If you wish to train seriously, you will need to base yourself in Spain, Portugal, southern France or parts of South America.

A bullfighter needs coordination, grace, strength and a sense of artistry. Needless to say, fearlessness is also pretty useful – both for facing the bull and carrying off the flamboyant outfit known as a *traje de luces* (suit of lights). To become a pro, you'll first need to be apprenticed to a master. The pay is poor, the hours long and the knocks plentiful. You will need to appear at small, local contests and build up a base of support. If you have the skill and perseverance, fame and serious money can beckon.

There is a lot of technical language to get to grips with. For starters, the bullfight itself is known as the *corrida*, the bullring as the *plaza de toros* and the bullfighter as a *torero* or matador.

Bullfights typically take place in the late afternoon and involve six bouts. Three matadors are given two bulls each, both weighing around 450 kilograms (1,000 lb). The contest has three distinct phases:
• *Tercio de varas* – where matador and bull face each other for the first time. The matador uses a magenta and gold cape to suss out how the bull moves and responds. A pair of horse-riding *picadors* then use spears to weaken the bull.
• *Tercio de banderillas* – three fighters on foot stab decorated, sharpened sticks (*banderillas*) into the bull's neck.
• *Tercio de muerte* – the matador taunts the bull by making passes with the classic, smaller red cape (*muleta*) before finally killing the creature with a curved sword. Of course, things don't always go according to plan, and it might be the matador who finds himself gored.

36 Become President of the United States

WHAT IT IS Taking over as the world's most powerful person
WHY YOU WON'T DO IT Washington politics is a dirty business

When Barack Obama moved into the White House in January 2008, he became the 44th president of the United States of America. And despite the constantly shifting sands of global influence, the US President remains pretty much the most powerful individual on the planet. It's a well-known truism that anyone can rise to this exalted office, so where should you start?

First, a few formalities. According to the Second Article of the US Constitution, in order to become president you must:
• Be a citizen born in the United States of America
• Be at least 35 years old (presumably the magical age at which you become imbued with wisdom)
• Have been resident in the USA or one of its dependent territories for the past 14 years.

If you still qualify, take a deep breath and ask yourself whether you really want the job – it's not all about being driven round in limos and meeting celebrities. Consider how you'd feel having your life thrown open to minute inspection by press and your political opponents, living under constant heavily armed guard and having the final say on decisions such as whether or not to launch nuclear missiles – all for the relatively humble salary of US$400,000 a year.

If you still want the job, consider whether you fit the typical presidential profile. Every president so far has been a man

– although Hilary Clinton came within a whisker of the Democratic candidacy in 2008, so perhaps times are changing. Harvard is the alma mater of choice for White House residents, and the average age of a president coming to power is just shy of 55.

More presidents have been registered as voters in New York than any other state (eight, to be precise), while eight were born in Virginia. Twenty-five have been lawyers by trade (the prime profession for aspiring presidents). Six were former career soldiers, while a further 25 had served spells in the armed forces. Fourteen served as vice president before moving up to the top job.

Once you start campaigning, you will need to be extraordinarily good at raising funds. According to some estimates, during the 2012 campaign Obama and his rival Mitt Romney spent almost US$6 billion between them. Primaries and caucuses to choose each party's candidate begin in January in the year of elections. New Hampshire is traditionally

IN GOD WE TRUST

AMERICAN ICON *Born in a one-room log cabin in 1809, Abraham Lincoln rose to become America's 16th president from 1861, and is perhaps the greatest embodiment of the American dream that anyone can be make it to the White House. Assassinated in 1865 by John Wilkes Booth, he remains an iconic figure for his part in ending slavery and for preserving the Union throughout the Civil War.*

Having secured your party's nomination at the national convention, appoint a running mate who appeals to a demographic you don't cover yourself. And remember, if you win but then die in office, they will take over – so try to make sure they're at least mildly competent.

In the run-up to the November election, get used to kissing a lot of babies, pressing a lot of flesh and above all avoiding gaffes. In 1992, vice presidential candidate Dan Quayle looked very silly when he misspelled 'potato' on a primary school visit. George W. Bush made a career out of similar slip-ups (but still managed to get elected, of course).

However much it pains you, make friends with the media, and don't have too much scandal in your background. In 1988 Gary Hart seemed assured of the Democrat ticket before allegations of infidelity with Donna Rice saw his campaign spectacularly derailed. That said, four years later Bill Clinton managed to shrug off allegations of an affair with model Gennifer Flowers. Clinton's ability to rise above the rumours and innuendo also bears out a famous dictum: 'it's the economy, stupid'. This was an idea popularized by Clinton campaign strategist James Carville. Whatever else is going on, people tend to be most worried about the dollar in their pocket.

Ultimately, remember that you need a clear majority in the electoral college – not necessarily a majority of the popular vote – so be strategic on your campaign trail. In 2000 George W. Bush famously won with less of the vote than his Democrat opponent, Al Gore.

And don't expect that life will get any easier once you're in office. As Thomas Jefferson once wryly noted: 'No man will ever bring out of the Presidency the reputation which carries him into it.'

the first to be held, and so generates massive media coverage. You don't want to do badly there as it has a reputation for making or breaking a campaign.

Campaigning is exhausting and not a good fit with home life. You will need an understanding family who support you in all your goals. Alongside them, gather together a brilliant team of advisers, speech writers, media figures and strategists (if you have seen *The West Wing*, think of President Jed Bartlet's killer team).

37

Negotiate a hostage release

WHAT IT IS Cutting a deal with kidnappers
WHY YOU WON'T DO IT It's a high-risk game requiring extraordinary personal skills and nerves of steel

Hostage negotiators undertake one of the most stressful jobs imaginable – trying to ensure that tense hostage stand-offs come to a peaceful conclusion. You will be put into high-pressure situations and must be able to think on your feet. You should also maintain a positive outlook to give yourself the best chance of securing a favourable outcome.

To become a professional negotiator, you will have to undertake a number of courses and secure the appropriate qualifications. But more important is a background in real-life crisis management. Law enforcement agencies are likely to be on the scene before your arrival. Get as much information from them as you can, but remember you are not one of them – your job is to be an intermediary, the calm centre of a web including hostage-takers, hostages and authorities.

Your first move is to find out who the hostage-taker is and what they want. Most situations are domestic, often involving a disturbed individual holding family members. The hostage-taker is likely to feel desperate and not in control, which can strengthen your position. Where the perpetrator has political aims, you stand less chance of 'talking them down'. Be prepared for negotiations to take hours, days or even more.

Never openly argue with the hostage-taker or refuse a demand, no matter how unreasonable. You don't want to risk losing lines of communication. Instead, meet a demand with a counter-offer. Most governments take a stance that striking deals with hostage-takers is unacceptable, but negotiating must by its nature include some room for manoeuvre.

In general, the longer a situation goes on, the more chance it will resolve itself well, so delay as much as you can. Don't ask questions with yes or no answers, and play for time by telling the hostage-taker that you have to clear their demands with a higher authority. Try to earn their trust and build up a psychological profile. Do whatever you can to ensure the well-being of the hostages. Try to get food and medical supplies to them if necessary. If you can secure the freedom of a few , then take the opportunity. As well as being out of danger, they will be able to supply information about what is going on at the scene and, in the event of an armed assault by law enforcement personnel, the fewer hostages the better.

Be an alchemist

38

WHAT IT IS Unlocking the secrets of manufacturing gold
WHY YOU WON'T DO IT Synthesis in any meaningful volume remains an elusive dream

The origins of alchemy date back to the great civilizations of antiquity, though it arguably reached its zenith in medieval Europe. Many souls devoted their lives to the pursuit of the philosopher's stone which, it was believed, had the properties to be able to confer immortality and transmute base metals into gold.

In its most advanced form, alchemy combined the burgeoning medieval knowledge of chemistry with a complex spiritual belief system. Its practitioners including famous men of science such as Tycho Brahe and Sir Isaac Newton. So far as we know, though, no one ever discovered the philosopher's stone itself – and if they did, we must assume they did not tell anybody and disappeared to live a life of quiet decadence on a yacht in the Mediterranean. So could you be the one who turns lead into gold?

If you want to go down the traditional route, study the plethora of books on the subject from throughout the ages. A dusty library is essential for any budding alchemist, as is a laboratory, replete with oddly shaped glassware and mysterious bubbling potions. But alchemy is not merely about chemicals – it is rich in symbolism, and requires that you go on a personal journey. Consider growing a long beard, through which you can run your fingers meaningfully while puzzling on the great mysteries of creation.

Today, however, modern physics and chemistry offer us a new kind of alchemy whose secrets lie with the capricious, fascinating but highly toxic liquid metal mercury. Gold and mercury are close chemical cousins – they sit next to each other on the periodic table of the elements, with 'atomic numbers' of 79 and 80 respectively. And under certain circumstances, mercury can indeed be transmuted into gold.

The similarity of the atomic numbers indicates that their individual atoms have similar structures. Mercury's higher number shows that it has one more positively charged particle (proton) and one more negatively charged electron than gold – strip these away and you've struck the yellow stuff. Scientists have demonstrated this in experiments that involved bombarding mercury atoms with high-energy particles in a nuclear reactor, although the costs of production far outweighed the market value of gold. So for the time being you're probably better off sticking with your glass retorts, test tubes and a pestle and mortar.

Find a natural pearl

39

WHAT IT IS One of nature's most stunning gifts
WHY YOU WON'T DO IT Naturally occurring pearls are few and far between

Humans have treasured pearls for more than 4,000 years. Indeed, Cleopatra once hosted 'the world's most expensive dinner party', during which she dissolved one of her finest pearls in a goblet of vinegary wine and drank it down. Today, however, the world's pearl trade deals almost exclusively in cultivated pearls and the natural variety are harder than ever to come by.

A pearl is an accident of nature, formed when an irritant, such as a parasite, lodges in the tissues of a mollusc (e.g. an oyster). The mollusc secretes a protective layer around the intruder made of nacre (a form of calcium carbonate). Over a number of years it builds up in layers to form a beautiful and iridescent pearl.

The poet John Dryden once wrote: 'Who would search for pearls must dive below.' Until about a century ago, pearls were found either by luck, or by specially trained divers who would open a great many oyster shells from the ocean floor in the hope of eventually finding a single pearl, often using the skills associated with free diving (see page 18). It was the danger and difficulty of obtaining pearls, as much as their iridescent beauty, that made them so valuable. Pearl fishing went on in many areas of the world, but is perhaps most associated with the Indian Ocean.

Then, in the early years of the 20th century, Japanese businessman Mikomoto Kokichi changed everything by developing a synthetic method of culturing pearls for the mass market. Ordinary people could finally afford them, though few would suggest that synthetic pearls compare in quality and lustre to their natural cousins.

Natural pearl diving in any organized form is rare today, although it still occurs off the coast of Bahrain and around Australia. The tradition also carries on in the United States around certain large rivers. To search for a natural pearl, you may need to dive to depths of 30 metres (100 ft) or more, with all the attendant risks. If you are going pearl diving, ensure you have sufficient training and experience, all the right equipment and a trustworthy companion to keep an eye on you.

You are likely to have to open upwards of a tonne's worth of shells to discover a haul of three or four pearls, but it could still be worth your while. In 2007, a double strand of natural pearls was auctioned for US$7 million.

40 Break a horse

WHAT IT IS Taming a wild spirit
WHY YOU WON'T DO IT This is not a trade that you can learn on the hoof

A process that sounds infinitely worse than it really is, breaking is the process of training a horse to accept riders and respond to their commands. The long-term chances of having a confident, responsive horse to ride are dependent on how successful the breaking is, and while there are various wildly differing techniques, ultimately they're all about communication.

You shouldn't even think about breaking a horse until it is around two years old, and at each stage you should make sure the animal is happy before moving on to the next. Your four-legged friend is going to be experiencing all manner of new experiences and feelings, and at the end of it all, you want it to have utter trust in you. So be prepared to take things slowly, over weeks or even months.

If possible, undertake the breaking process in partnership with a trainer and an assistant. The first stage involves attaching an extended 'lunge line' to the halter around the horse's head. Lead it around the pen, introducing simple commands such as 'whoa', 'walk' and 'back'. Lavish praise when things go well and don't lose patience when they don't. If you think the horse is getting tired or fed up, finish your session for the day.

Once the horse is able to follow these commands, you can start to introduce riding paraphernalia. Get it used to wearing a bridle and bit, and feeling the stirrups hanging by its side. You can eventually introduce the saddle too. The horse may find this heavy, alien object disconcerting at first, but persevere.

Some riders now drape themselves over the saddle so that they are lying across the horse. This allows for a quick and safe exit, while getting the horse used to the weight of a rider. The next stage is to actually sit on the horse – get your feet in the stirrups but keep your weight off the saddle. While offering plenty of comfort and praise, ease your full weight into the saddle. If your mount remains calm, try walking a few paces before halting.

Once on horseback, the temptation grows to push on but don't get ahead of yourself; a little every day remains the rule. Start backing up verbal commands with appropriate actions. To walk, give a gentle nudge with your legs. To halt, pull gently on the reins. Work hard to associate spoken commands with physical cues. When the horse is ready, remove the lunge line and start building your relationship as rider and horse – this is where the real work begins!

41 Train a falcon

WHAT IT IS Bringing a
bird of prey under
your control
WHY YOU WON'T DO IT
The bonds of trust between
man and bird take an age
to establish

It's easy to understand the attraction of falconry, the ancient sport of hunting wild prey with a trained hawk. It is, however, a pastime that requires immense reserves of dedication, not to mention time and money. No wonder it's a sport that's traditionally been the preserve of royalty and the nobility.

One of the first things you'll need to look into is your legal situation – check local laws governing the ownership and upkeep of birds of prey, as well as legislation concerning hunting and game. You may well have to pass formal exams and will almost certainly need to apply for specific licences. Do your research, read as many books as you can, undertake practical courses and ask the advice of experienced falconers – hawks are not household pets.

In the USA, novice falconry is limited to red-tailed hawks or American kestrels. Meanwhile, the British Falconers' Club recommends that beginners start with either a red-tailed or a Harris hawk. Beginners' birds are almost always captive-bred. You'll have to provide suitable accommodation (a 'mews'), and need a range of equipment that includes jesses (leather straps for the legs), a swivel and leash to secure the bird, bells, a hood to keep the bird calm (especially during early training), an identity tag and a perch, and most importantly from your own point of view, heavy gloves.

Your first job is to 'man' the bird, getting it used to humans. Encourage it to fly to your (gloved) fist with a tasty morsel of meat. Make a distinctive sound with the lips or tongue, or whistle as the bird eats, so it associates that particular noise with food. Once a bond of trust is formed, you can introduce it to the disturbances of the wider world, such as dogs, traffic and other people.

Once the bird will eat happily from the glove, you can introduce the creance, a longer line, and train your bird to return to hand immediately from perches up to 30 metres (100 ft) away. The next stage is to train with a lure – a leather weight on a rope to which food can be attached. As you get more adept at swinging the lure, you will be able to experience the bird making dramatic approaches from long distances, swooping past at high speeds.

Finally, you are ready for free flight. This is when the bird is completely untethered and could fly away to freedom. At this point, many falconers fit their birds with radio-tracking transmitters just in case!

106 LOST ARTS AND UNUSUAL PROFESSIONS

42 Tie yourself in knots

WHAT IT IS The noble art of contortionism
WHY YOU WON'T DO IT How rubbery is your spine?

It's not everyone's cup of tea, but if you have occasionally thought how much you'd like to be able to sit on your own shoulders, then there is probably a contortionist's spirit trapped within you and just waiting to bend its way out. To become a contortionist you'll need dedication, patience and physical prowess.

Contortionists achieve their remarkable feats by hyperflexing or hyperextending their spines – it's all about teaching the body to do something that it doesn't naturally want to do. Your body will be able to get into poses that constantly surprise you but be prepared for some to be beyond you. And don't forget to enjoy it – contortion is a great way of relieving stress. You can learn the skills at any age, but it's generally accepted that the younger you are, the easier it will be.

Start slowly, getting into a routine of daily stretches to build a level of flexibility and suppleness into your body. Yoga is also beneficial. It's worth preparing yourself for a good month before trying anything serious, and once you start training in earnest, you should still do at least 15 minutes of warm-up before trying anything serious. Take extra care about what you consume. Lots of fruit and veg is great but eat meat in moderation, and make sure it's lean – you'll want to keep your body fat at a safe minimum. Drink lots of water, but don't eat anything in the hour or two before a session.

Give yourself plenty of space and make sure your training area is cool and airy. To get to a professional standard, expect to do three hours of training per day, ideally over three sessions (morning, afternoon and evening).Try not to miss any sessions – some say that even a day off can set your progress back by a week. Work with a partner. Not only is it more fun but it is also safer – they can check that you are doing particular exercises in the right way, spotting, for instance, whether you're using your whole spine or putting all the strain on a few vertebrae.

Contortionists generally come in two flavours, evocatively known as frontbenders and backbenders, but try to develop a full and varied act: frontbenders often incorporate backbending exercises and vice versa. You might also include some splits and oversplits (a split of more than 180 degrees). Whatever you do, don't endanger yourself – contortionism is quite literally about stretching yourself to the limit, but don't push yourself so far that you do yourself a mischief.

Fish for Alaskan king crab

WHAT IT IS A challenge to get your claws into
WHY YOU WON'T DO IT There are easier ways to get your dinner

The red king crab is the most valuable of all the king crab and inhabits the waters at depths between 35 and 180 metres (120–600 ft). Historically, fishing for these prized crustaceans in the Bering Sea off Alaska has been the most profitable job a commercial fisherman can aspire too, but there's good reason for that – it's about as dangerous as fishing can get.

In good times, a crew member on a king crab boat can hope to make a six-figure salary over the course of a year. However, the US Bureau of Labor Statistics rates commercial fishing as the most dangerous of all occupations, with a fatality rate 90 times higher than the American average, at 300 per 100,000. Leading causes of death include hypothermia, drowning and industrial accidents. Despite there still being much money to be made, wholesale prices have declined since the boom years of the 1980s. The days when a boat owner could make millions in a single season are over.

The centre of the king crab industry is Alaska's Bristol Bay, so you'll need to relocate to this beautiful but harsh region. The many salmon fishing boats that operate in the same area will help you gain experience and stay solvent while you wait for your break on a crab boat. Check that your paperwork is all in order – fishermen are expected to have their own licences (roughly US$65 for Alaskan residents, US$165 for everyone

else). Make sure yours is good to go so that you can act as soon as an opening arises – unsurprisingly, competition for these highly paid jobs is ferocious.

Vacancies don't tend to be advertized, with news of job opportunities spreading by word of mouth – your best hope is to be in the right place at the right time, and to keep an ear to the ground. Train yourself to network. And if you find out about a job, move quickly.

Regardless of what other experience you have, if you're new on the crab boats you'll be at the bottom of the pecking order. You'll assume the status of a novice and will be referred to as a 'greenhorn'. Greenhorns very often undertake their first trip for no pay; if you can prove yourself, the rewards will follow later.

Stay tough, and keep yourself in good physical condition: awful storms might break at any moment, and you'll certainly have to deal with extremes of cold in the subarctic conditions of the

KING FISHERS *A trawler battles the rough and icy seas of the Bering Strait in pursuit of the prized crustaceans at the opening of the Bristol Bay red king crab season off the coast of Alaska. The job is dangerous, the conditions are miserable, but the rewards are potentially huge.*

Bering Sea. In fact, it's often so cold that water freezes on the decks, making every aspect of manoeuvring around the boat a challenge. You're likely to spend a good deal of time chipping ice off your vessel, and should make sure you wear gloves at all times to avoid accidentally freezing yourself to anything. There is also a lot of seriously heavy equipment moving about, which just adds to the danger.

Prepare to work and live in very cramped conditions, with shifts lasting anything up to 48 hours. In years gone by, the fishing season lasted for only three or four days, so up to 250 boats would race for the prime fishing spots in a sort of derby. These days there are fewer boats (reflecting reduced stock levels), but the season is longer, with some boats on the water for three or four weeks at a time. The crabs tend to gather in the coldest water near the edge of ice shelves.

Crabs are caught in huge steel-framed pots weighing 360 kilograms (800 lb)

each and baited with cod or herring. There may be 300 of these pots on a typical boat, lowered and raised from the sea by hydraulic winches. Once a catch has been sorted, the king crabs are stored alive in a holding tank.

Crab fishing is heavily regulated. There is a strictly observed fishing season, and only male specimens of a certain size can be landed, with smaller crabs and females returned to the sea in order to maintain stocks. Quotas are calculated on a season-by-season and boat-by-boat basis, and failure to adhere to the strict rules can be punished with fines of hundreds of thousands of dollars for boat owners.

Oh, and there's one other unusual bonus – each season Discovery Channel's hit TV show *Deadliest Catch* follows the boats out to sea on the lookout for new reality TV stars – so if you're in the right place at the right time, you might find the fisherman's life leads to unexpected fame as well as fortune.

44 # Become a submariner

WHAT IT IS Life beneath the ocean waves
WHY YOU WON'T DO IT Aside from the claustrophobia, it's a killer for your social life

Anyone who has read Jules Verne's *Twenty Thousand Leagues Under the Sea* or watched *Das Boot* is unlikely to feel entirely confident about rushing off to become a submariner. Nonetheless, there still seem to be plenty of hardy souls who hear the calling to lock themselves in a small tin can and live on the ocean floor – maybe you're one of them?

Today, submarines have a wide variety of uses ranging from tourism through oil exploration to oceanographic study. However, the most common way to become a submariner is still by joining your country's navy.

They'll put you through a vigorous programme of training, testing you to make sure you're physically, psychologically and temperamentally suited to the job: if you've got even a whiff of claustrophobia about you, it'll be found out and you'll be restricted to surface operations. Try to remember it's for your own good – you're going to be in a small space that you can't leave for weeks or even months at a time. To give you an idea of what you might face, a Royal Navy Trafalgar Class boat (submarines are always 'boats', never 'ships') is only 85 metres (280 ft) long, 10 metres (33 ft) high and 10 metres (33 ft) wide, and it has to function as home and workplace for 130 men for six months at a stretch. It all sounds a lot less jolly than, say, living with the Beatles on their famous Yellow Submarine.

Fortunately, seasickness tends not to be too much of a problem – you might think that bumping along at the bottom of the sea would guarantee nausea, but in fact the water down there is considerably calmer than it is on the surface.

A submarine requires all sorts of specialist professions on board, from engineers to cooks. It is vital that everyone works in harmony at all times, and because of the peculiar demands upon them, naval submariners are almost always volunteers, even in wartime. In virtually every navy, submariners are male only. This can lead to a certain level of tension and, dare it be said, 'frustration' among crew. The average age of a submariner is 21. Relationships are, not surprisingly, difficult to keep going underwater. Marriage breakdown is not uncommon among submariners.

You'll also have to cope with boredom, although you should at least have plenty of opportunity to catch that film you missed at the cinema or finally finish

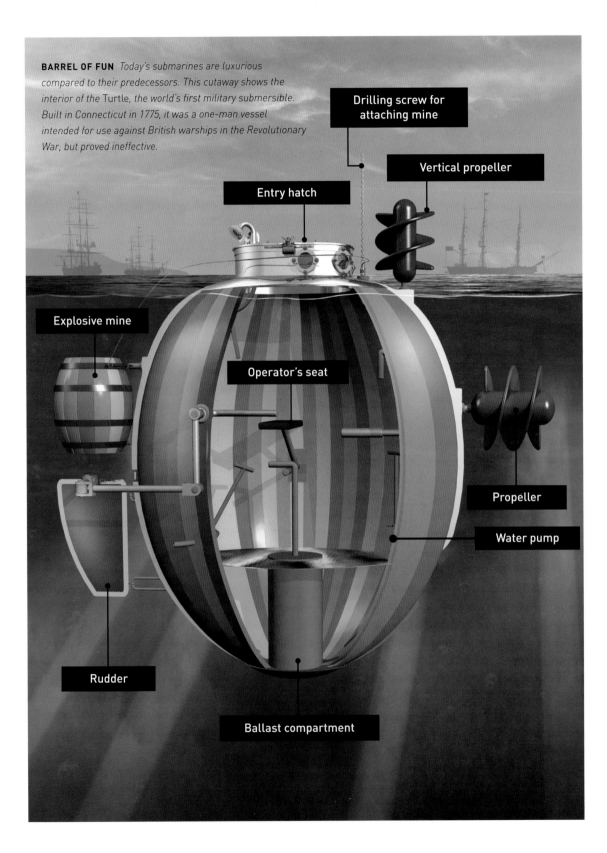

BARREL OF FUN *Today's submarines are luxurious compared to their predecessors. This cutaway shows the interior of the Turtle, the world's first military submersible. Built in Connecticut in 1775, it was a one-man vessel intended for use against British warships in the Revolutionary War, but proved ineffective.*

Drilling screw for attaching mine

Vertical propeller

Entry hatch

Explosive mine

Operator's seat

Propeller

Water pump

Rudder

Ballast compartment

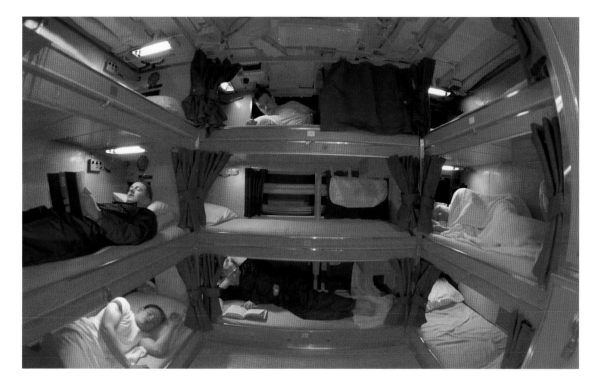

TIN OF SARDINES *Crew members relax in their bunks aboard the Ohio-class nuclear submarine USS Alabama – the red light provides safe levels of constant illumination without disrupting sleep. It might not be spacious, but it's a lot more comfortable than conditions aboard the early submersible* Turtle *(shown opposite), used against British ships in the War of Independence.*

that book (ideally not *The Hunt for Red October*). You will probably work a regimented shift pattern of six hours on and six hours off. Four meals are served a day, with the crew usually managing to eat at two of the sittings. Due to the absence of space for exercise, many submariners complain of putting on weight during a voyage.

To save space, bunks are normally stacked in threes. Your privacy (what there is of it) is preserved by a curtain, and aside from your bunk, you might only have a shelf or locker to call your own. If you're unlucky you may even have to 'hot bunk' – grabbing whichever bunk comes free at the shift changeover. What's

more, fresh water is at a premium so you may have to go for several days, or even weeks, without showering.

For security reasons, communication with the outside world is minimal, although satellite technology makes it possible to keep in contact with vessels virtually anywhere. A captain will often have to decide whether a submariner should be told some bad news while he is powerless to do anything about it.

While modern submarines have every safety provision imaginable, disasters can still happen: in 2000, for instance, the Russian sub K-141 *Kursk* sunk in the Barents Sea with the loss of all 118 hands. If something goes really wrong down there, you are in trouble. So if you're determined to travel in a sub, why not take an easier option than joining the navy? If you have deep pockets, you could fork out for a trip to see the wreck of the *Titanic* in a sub. Prices start at around US$60,000 per person.

45 Perform brain surgery

WHAT IT IS A literal case of getting inside the human mind
WHY YOU WON'T DO IT Only the brightest, most driven and hardest-working need apply

The modern field of neurosurgery involves preventing, diagnosing and treating disorders related to the brain, spinal column, spinal cord and peripheral nerves. Becoming a neurosurgeon requires a heady mix of skill, intelligence, dexterity, stamina and perseverance – small wonder that brain surgery has become a byword for difficulty.

The brain is the most complex of any organ in the body. For starters, it is made up of some 10 billion neurons with over 13 trillion connections. That's a lot to get to grips with, and not surprisingly, if you want to become a neurosurgeon you can expect to undertake an immense amount of training. In the first instance, you'll need a good basic medical degree. Competition is fierce to even get a place at medical school – you will need top-notch exam results, proven interest in the field, and evidence of good character.

Once your degree finishes, the real hard work begins. Neurosurgery tends to attract the crème de la crème, so the pressure to shine only increases. You will carry out a series of placements and spend years as a resident. Neurosurgery is such a fast-moving field of medicine that you'll be constantly studying just to keep your knowledge up to date. At the end, perhaps 14 years after leaving school, expect to finish your training in considerable debt, but with qualifications that will help you earn some of the biggest bucks in the medical profession.

As well as being academically brilliant, you also need a steady hand. You will be undertaking long and very delicate procedures and, quite simply, you won't be up to the job if you have sausage fingers! You should also be comfortable with new technology. Surgeons today use all manner of imaging equipment, micro-cameras and robotic devices and you must feel confident with all of them.

You are unlikely to keep regular hours. Brain surgeons are not two-a-penny so expect to be on call at all hours and be ready to come into work at short notice. The job can also be emotionally testing – the futures of people suffering from brain tumours and trauma injuries will literally be in your hands. Sadly, some will be beyond your help so you will also have to know when to give up the fight. The up-side is that outcomes are now better than ever before. Improvements in diagnosis and surgical practices have led to quicker and less invasive surgery, while fatality rates have fallen from some 50 per cent in the mid-20th century to less than 10 per cent today.

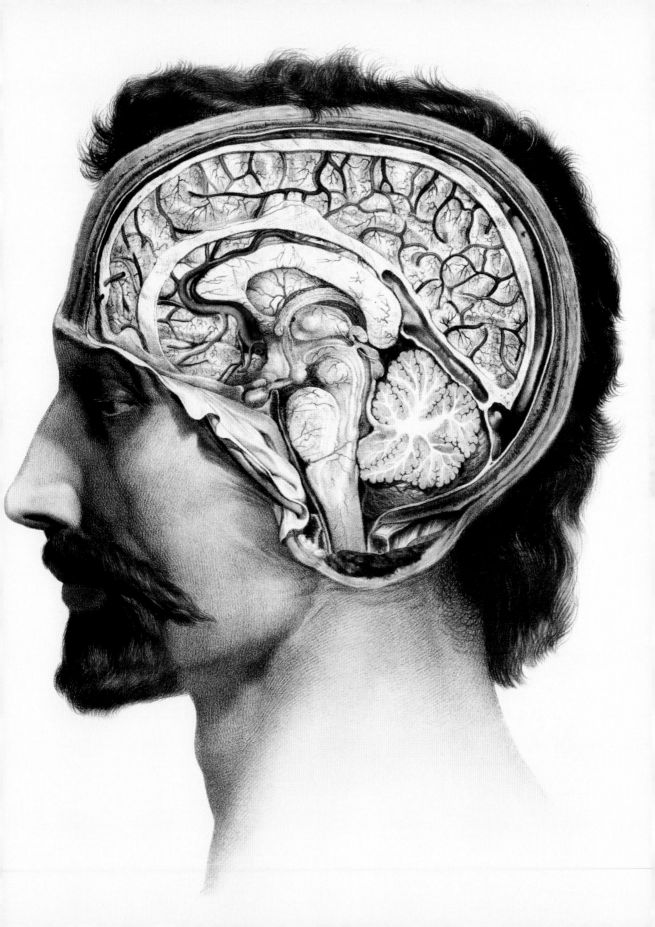

46 Find a cure for cancer

WHAT IT IS Perhaps the ultimate medical Holy Grail
WHY YOU WON'T DO IT Cancers are many and varied, and the science behind them is complex

In 1971 the US President, Richard Nixon, predicted that scientists would find a cure for cancer within five years. As we know, that sadly never happened. Twenty-eight years later, President Obama pledged US$6 billion towards reaching the same goal 'in our time' – but is even that really achievable?

Every day, it seems, newspapers splash headlines suggesting that the elusive 'cure for cancer' might be just around the corner, but perhaps unsurprisingly, such sensationalized news stories rarely give the full picture. The main issue is that while cancer is often spoken of as if it were a single monolithic challenge, in medical terms it is a catch-all term for a wide range of related diseases that involve cells in various parts of the body mutating and beginning to divide and grow uncontrollably. So while it's true that cancer treatments are constantly developing, even the biggest breakthroughs tend to promise victories in specific battles rather than the end of the war itself.

There are an estimated 1.5 million new cancer cases each year in the USA alone, and the search to find an effective and reliable 'one size fits all' cure is one of the Holy Grails of medicine. But there are many who believe that the answer lies in other approaches. To join the frontline of the battle, you will need to qualify as an oncologist – the arm of the medical profession specializing in cancer. Needless to say, you will have to complete an arduous basic medical degree before specializing in your chosen field and then undertaking several more years of on-the-job study.

While you will be doing amazing work that can improve and prolong the lives of patients, you will also be exposed to massive stress, dealing with people at very low points in their lives and sometimes having to conclude that their battles cannot be won.

The most commonly used treatments today – surgery, chemotherapy and radiotherapy – have good and improving rates of success, but no one would go as far as to claim that they represent a complete solution. In addition, any of them can lead to unpleasant side effects for the patient. As a result, many oncologists favour a slightly different focus, geared towards learning how to better *manage* cancers. That is to say, some scientists aspire to a time when cancers that are now fatal will instead

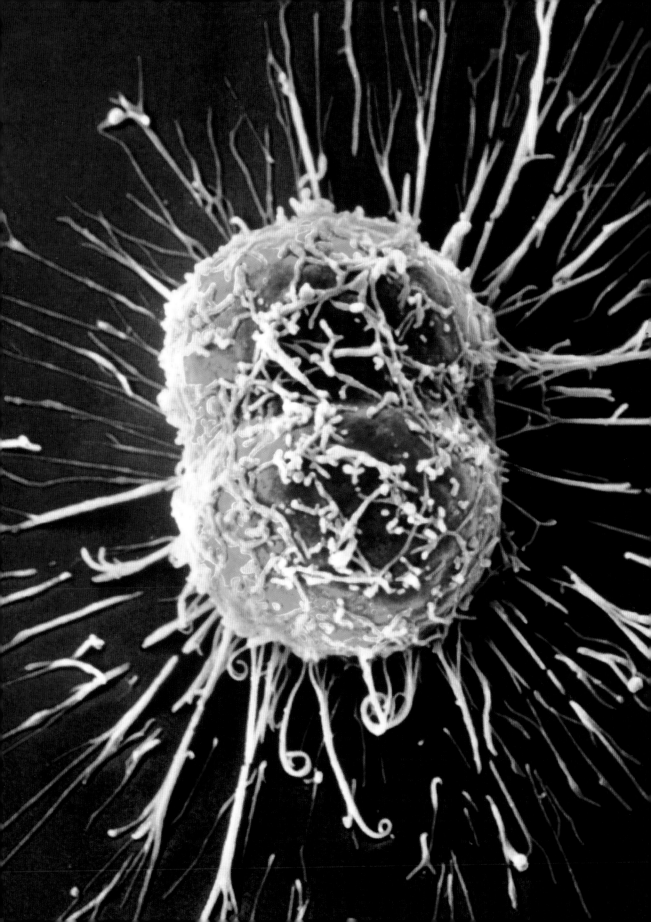

THE NOBLE FIGHT *A scientist studies a plate comprising more than 20,000 pieces of DNA related to Chromosome 17 and linked to breast cancer. Ongoing development in the understanding of genes offers one of the brightest hopes for finding more ways to effectively combat cancer.*

if you smoke, while overexposure to the sun increases the likelihood of skin cancer. Other cancers can be aggravated by dietary factors and particular environmental conditions. So many oncologists favour educating people about lifestyle choices in the hope of preventing new cancer cases, rather than spending billions on pharmaceutical research in the hope of turning up a miracle drug that may well not exist. Would it not be better, the theory goes, to spend more of our finite resources on, say, educating sunbathers in safe practices so that new instances of skin cancer are reduced?

Addressing infections could also have a huge role in future cancer treatments. For instance, it is clear that hepatitis can have links to liver cancer, while the bacteria that causes peptic ulcers can also provoke stomach cancer. Currently, cancers stemming at least partly from infections account for an estimated 15–20 per cent of all cases, but some researchers believe that by 2050 that figure could be as high as 95 per cent. In a bid to gain a foothold within the human body, certain viruses have effectively broken down our natural barriers to cancer; it should be possible to counter some of these through a combination of improved hygiene and greater use of vaccinations and antibiotics.

Another avenue for research involves improving on the body's natural defences – several groups of scientists are currently striving to develop 'super' white blood cells which, it is hoped, will be able to blitz cancerous cells. Another innovative approach, announced in 2010, uses light-activated compounds that work to make cancerous cells self-destruct. This could potentially offer a means of highly effective treatment without the side effects inherent in current methods.

be regarded as 'chronic illnesses' – conditions that are serious but largely controllable, similar to diabetes. There are at least 200 distinct forms of cancer, so it seems unlikely that there will be a single drug that combats them all. That said, there are still plenty of people who believe that certain cancers might eventually be controlled by pharmaceuticals.

It's also well known that lifestyle can have an impact on certain cancers – you're at higher risk of lung cancer

Become a spy

WHAT IT IS Delving into the murky world of espionage
WHY YOU WON'T DO IT It takes more than an encyclopedic knowledge of the Bond movies

Who hasn't watched a James Bond film at one time or another and thought that they could do his job just as well? The truth, though, is that the world of espionage is not often as action-packed as it's portrayed in the movies – but that's not to say that it isn't a career to test you to the limits.

Spying has sometimes been described as the world's second-oldest profession. It goes on between countries, companies and even couples. If you work for a national intelligence agency, such as the CIA in the United States or the Secret Intelligence Service (MI6) in the UK, you could be helping to disrupt terrorism, maintain the global power balance and perhaps secure peace in war-torn regions of the world. Sadly, however, you probably *won't* be doing it while out-skiing avalanches or dodging steel-rimmed bowler hats. So what are the intelligence agencies looking for?

The principal role of a spy is to collect, evaluate and disseminate intelligence that others are trying to keep secret. In essence, you're providing the necessary information for policy-makers to decide how your government should act. There will be immense mental and emotional demands upon you (and sometimes physical demands as well). If an 'ordinary' life is your goal, then espionage is probably not the right career for you.

Acting in the interests of your country may also mean doing things that make you feel ethically uncomfortable. You will almost certainly have to lie or at least conceal things from your friends and loved ones – which is quite a test for even the strongest relationship. And even if you're comfortable with all that, getting a position is still no easy task. There are three main routes in:
• Security services will often have a presence at the best universities to identify those with suitable minds and temperaments for the job. If you've ever read a John Le Carré novel, you know the sort of thing – a potential spy may be approached by a representative of the service and invited to apply for a post.
• Occasionally, someone will offer their services unsolicited and be recruited because they offer the possibility of access to useful intelligence. For instance, a disgruntled diplomat may offer to spy on his own government.
• More commonly these days, however, vacancies are simply advertized like any other job, and prospective spies go through a standard application process.

LOST ARTS AND UNUSUAL PROFESSIONS

SPY CRAFT *Lest we thought that espionage had died at the end of the Cold War, Russian authorities claimed in 2006 that British diplomatic staff had been using this fake rock, stuffed with electronic equipment, as a tool in a concerted spying campaign.*

If taking the latter route, it helps to have a solid academic background – science, IT, economics, psychology and political theory are all particularly useful, and fluency in one or more foreign languages can be a great boon, especially if they are spoken in a current 'hot spot'. For instance, following the 9/11 attacks, speakers of Arabic languages were particularly in demand.

The intelligence services will subject you to extensive background checks, so make sure you live a clean life. You should have no criminal record, no history of financial problems and no embarrassing relations – if your uncle worked for the KGB, that could be a problem unless you're after a job at its successor, the FSB. Essentially, you should have nothing that could be used by enemies to influence your actions or blackmail you. In addition, a clean record suggests you have a reasonably balanced temperament and haven't drawn undue attention to yourself. You have more chance of being recruited if you are under 35 years old. You must be willing to do a lot of travel, to be away from home for long periods and perhaps even to relocate permanently.

Recruiters are looking for people who demonstrate calmness under pressure, have the ability to quickly analyse (both people and information), are able to manipulate others to obtain information, have the skills to adapt to changing circumstances and can maintain a false identity. Also useful are the ability to write well (you will be filing a lot of field reports) and physical fitness (if you need to extricate yourself from a tricky situation). Most important of all is the ability to stick to the task at hand and see it through to successful completion. Beware, the pay is probably not as good as you might hope. In general, you are looking at five figures rather than six.

And if all that sounds a bit too corporate, then romantics might like to know that the good old days of 'eyeholes in newspapers' are not altogether over. In 2006, British agents were filmed passing secrets via a fake rock located in a Moscow park. Just don't push your luck by asking for a licence to kill or an Aston Martin with an ejector seat.

48 | Charm a snake

WHAT IT IS Persuading
a serpent to dance to
your tune
WHY YOU WON'T DO IT
People and snakes have
struggled to work together
since the days of Adam
and Eve

'Hypnotizing' a venomous snake might seem like a risky business, but snake charmers are wily fellows who do everything in their power to eliminate danger. Though the practice is now outlawed in India, there are still around a million charmers, most of whom learned the skill from their fathers. So what's the secret?

The first thing you'll need to do if you're seriously considering a career in snake charming is to find out whether it's even legal in your part of the world. It's forbidden in many parts of the world for protection of both the animals involved and their rapidly declining environment.

Assuming you're in the clear, the first thing you'll need to do is get a snake. A cobra is the classic choice, but a viper will do just as well. In all honesty, get somebody with specialist skills to obtain the snake for you, and make sure it's from a legitimate source.

Snake charming is not a profession beloved of the animal rights movement for good reason. It is not uncommon for charmers to remove the snake's fangs or venom glands, and in some cases, to actually sew the snake's mouth closed. None of these methods are recommended here, but 'milking' the snake to temporarily drain its venom seems like a good idea. Once again, though, you should get a specialist rather than do it yourself.

Put the snake in a pot or basket, don a suitably 'mystic' outfit and find a spot in a crowded market. Lay down your basket/pot and sit by it in a cross-legged pose, out of biting range just in case. (As a rule of thumb, a cobra's attack range is about one-third of its body length). Keep the snake well fed so it is likely to be docile. When you take the lid off the pot/basket, the snake will probably 'stand up' without encouragement – a defensive rather than aggressive gesture, and hardly surprising given the circumstances.

Start playing your flute, while swaying the instrument from side to side. The snake appears to 'dance' to it. In fact, they do not hear music like humans do. Instead, they respond to the sight of the moving instrument – no hypnosis required. At the end of the act, slowly replace the lid on the container. But in retrospect, why not take the snake out of the equation altogether and just learn to play the flute really well instead? It's a lot kinder to animals and if you get really good, it could earn you a lot more money.

50 Wrestle an alligator

WHAT IT IS Toughing it out with one of nature's most fearsome beasts
WHY YOU WON'T DO IT It's a fight you could only hope to have once

You know the old joke about not annoying an alligator because they can be a bit snappy? There are only a handful of fatalities from alligator attacks in any one year in the United States so it's important not to live in fear of such a rare event – but if you do get caught in a 'gator dust-up, there is probably only going to be one winner.

The alligator's natural habitat is tropical, swampy areas. They are not going to go out of their way to make trouble for you, but if you're hanging around in their 'hood, they may consider you fair game. These ancient reptiles are at their most active during warm summer months, and the most dangerous time for attacks is at dusk and in the early evening. If you find yourself in alligator territory, do your best not to attract their attention. For instance, if you're on a fishing trip, don't clean fish in the water. Perhaps surprisingly, golfers are also in particular peril – if you hit an awful shot and end up in the water, think very carefully before wading in to recover your lost ball. And if you're out in the wilds with a favourite pet, keep them away from the water's edge. Regardless of how faithful Fido is, to an alligator he's just a tasty snack.

If you see 'no swimming' signs, pay attention, and don't rely on your ability to spot an alligator – they are wily ambush predators who can maintain a very low profile in the water when they want to.

If you're on land and have a head start, you can try outrunning an alligator – they have a mighty turn of speed but are not keen on prolonged land pursuits.

In the water you can forget about out-swimming your opponent, so if you realize you've attracted some unwanted attention, make as much of a commotion as possible. By making a nuisance of yourself, you might convince the alligator you're just too much trouble

If you become engaged in a physical struggle, fight back. The alligator will attempt to drag you beneath the surface and pull you into a death roll. Hit the alligator where it hurts – go for the eyes, nostrils and ears, poking them with fingers or any weapon you can find. Try to cut them, or hit them as hard as you possibly can. To stop an alligator drowning underwater, it has a flap of tissue at the back of the throat behind the tongue. If the creature has managed to get its jaws around your limbs, aim for this flap with an arm or leg in the hope that it will instinctively release you.

51 See a Yangtze River dolphin

WHAT IT IS Among the world's most endangered species
WHY YOU WON'T DO IT Their numbers are tiny and rapidly decreasing – if there are any left at all

Native only to the Yangtze River in China, this beautiful dolphin (also known as the *baiji*) is one of only four freshwater dolphin species in the world, having headed off down a specialized evolutionary cul-de-sac around 20 million years ago. Once venerated as the 'Goddess of the Yangtze', it has more recently fallen victim mankind's abuse of the planet's natural resources.

Yangtze River dolphins have a distinctive white colour, with a longer, thinner beak than their saltwater cousins, and a low dorsal fin. They live in small groups of just three or four, feeding on fish. In the 1950s the mighty river was home to a reasonably healthy population of 6,000, but by 1997 the number had declined to fewer than 50. The last confirmed sighting of one was in 2004, and in 2006 a team of scientists on two research vessels spent over six weeks searching for the dolphins but found none at all.

Listed as 'critically endangered' by the World Conservation Union, other scientists have classified the species as 'functionally extinct'. This means that while there is a possibility that a small number of animals are still alive, there are too few to ensure successful breeding and ward off extinction. Previous attempts to breed the dolphins in captivity proved unsuccessful, and if the species is indeed extinct, it will be the first large invertebrate to die out since the Caribbean monk seal died out in the 1950s.

The blame for this sad decline lies squarely with humanity. Among the leading reasons for the dolphin's decline are unregulated fishing (with dolphins regularly falling prey to hooks and nets), collisions with river vessels (many equipped with fast-spinning and potentially lethal propellers), persistent environmental degradation and pollution, and disruption to the dolphins' patterns of movement by the development of the waterways. The already-beleaguered dolphin even became a target for hunting and human consumption for a few years around 1960.

However, there was a very slight ray of hope in 2007 when video footage emerged of what appeared to be a Yangtze dolphin. So if you travel to China and spend long enough scouring the waters, you might just get lucky – and maybe even earn your own footnote in the annals of natural history. But the future for the species remains bleak, and so, tragically, scientists are mostly left to study preserved remains in a select number of institutions around the world.

52 Capture a giant squid

WHAT IT IS A veritable monster from below the waves
WHY YOU WON'T DO IT For something so large, they are great at keeping a low profile

Giant squid first crop up in the writings of the ancient Greek Aristotle, and are believed to have inspired the kraken, the fearsome sea monster of Norse mythology. They have enchanted the minds of writers ever since, terrorizing sailors in *Moby Dick* and *20,000 Leagues Under the Sea* – but no one has yet managed to snare a live one.

If you encounter the giant squid (Latin name: *Architeuthis dux*) at close quarters, you'll have little problem recognizing it. Specimens measure up to 13 metres (43 ft) from caudal fin to tentacle tip, and weigh up to several hundred kilograms. By the mid-2000s there were some 600 preserved specimens in institutions around the world.

The squid has some of the hugest eyes in the natural world, measuring 30 centimetres (12 in) across, to absorb the little light available in the depths of the ocean. Their strong, beak-like mouths can sever through metal cables, while suckers on their tentacles snare prey and pull it to its doom.

So why are these awesome invertebrates so elusive? The reason is that they spend virtually all of their lives in the deepest, darkest parts of the ocean, at depths between 300 and 1,000 metres (1,000–3,300 ft). There are thought to be sizeable populations in all the world's oceans.In the 19th century, particularly

large numbers of squid were washed ashore around Newfoundland and New Zealand. Fairly regular sightings continue in both of these locations, as well as around the coast of Australia, the northern British Isles, Japan, Norway, Spain and Southern Africa. If you're determined to land yourself one, your geographical location is among the least of your problems.

Some would suggest that your best bet is to find a nice spot on a beach in one of the areas above and wait for the tide to bring a carcass ashore. This method, however, demonstrates a singular lack of spirit. Furthermore, washed-up specimens are usually in a pretty unpleasant state.

So assuming you want to catch a live one, you might attract its attention of by sailing around in a tanker. It's not known whether the squid mistakes tankers for an enemy or a potential supper dish, but there are records of one Norwegian tanker that was attacked on three separate occasions in the 1930s.

54 Survive a Komodo dragon attack

WHAT IT IS A fearsome creature with prehistoric credentials
WHY YOU WON'T DO IT Death by Komodo is a slow and gruesome process

Often nicknamed 'the land crocodile', the Komodo dragon is actually a giant monitor lizard, but it's still not the sort of creature that you want to bump into up a dark alley. Fortunately, there's little chance of that unless you are on one of a small number of Indonesian islands – but how would you cope in a chance encounter?

Native to the Southeast Asian islands of Komodo, Rinca, Flores, Gili Motang and Gili Dasami, the Komodo (*Varanus komodoensis*) has been wandering the earth for upwards of 4 million years. Today there are about 4,000 animals left. They can grow to more than 3 metres (10 ft) long, and weigh in at more than 100 kilograms (220 lb). A yellow forked tongue is one of their most distinctive features, and key to their remarkable sense of smell – their primary weapon in sniffing out dinner.

Although able to sprint fast over short distances, dragons are ambush predators, preferring to lie in stealth before launching a sudden attack on prey that can range from wild boar and buffalo to snakes and birds. Having lunged with great speed, the Komodo grabs its victim between powerful jaws lined with serrated, shark-like teeth. Often the prey will survive the initial attack, but even if it escapes, it is almost certainly doomed by the dragon's first deep bite. For many years, the potency of this bite was attributed to a cocktail

of bacteria in its saliva, so the 2009 discovery that Komodos are actually venomous came as something of a surprise. It's now clear that a dragon's toxic bite causes a rapid drop in blood pressure, prevents blood clotting and swiftly sends the victim into shock. Thereafter, the dragon will happily track its victim over long distances and for several days if necessary, wearing it down. As other dragons get the scent of the dying animal, a crowd may gather to feast on the carcass.

Fortunately, fatal attacks on humans are rare. An eight-year-old boy killed in 2007 was the first recorded death in 33 years. Nevertheless, a hungry dragon will sometimes launch an unprovoked attack on a human – and more attacks happen on Rinca than any other island. Dragons can run at speeds of 20 kilometres per hour (12 mph) and are also strong swimmers, limiting your chances of escape. Instead, you may have to stand and fight, so it's worth keeping a weapon such as a knife close at hand in danger areas. If you are attacked, stab at the

56 Sneeze with your eyes open

WHAT IT IS A challenge to overcome your natural instincts
WHY YOU WON'T DO IT If it's something you're hardwired to do, why fight it?

Technically speaking, a sneeze is known as a 'sternutatory reflex' – the body's ingenious way of giving your nose and sinuses a good clear out. But try and think about what you see when you sneeze – is it nothing? That's because, unless you are one of a small minority, you can't do it with your eyes open.

The urge to sneeze starts to build when an irritant comes into contact with the mucous membranes lining your nostrils. This causes histamines to irritate the nose's nerve cells, precipitating a series of reactions in the brain that eventually result in the sneeze, which expels a mixture of oxygen, mucus and foreign particles.

The power of a sneeze should not be underestimated – although it's a difficult thing to accurately measure and varies greatly from person to person, a typical sneeze can briefly generate a blast of air travelling at between 160 and 320 kilometres per hour (100 and 200 mph). Indeed, Dr Alfred Kinsey, the great American pioneer of sex research, once likened the orgasm to the act of sneezing.

The action of sneezing puts your entire body under stress. It has long been said by some mischievous types that if we didn't close our eyes during the process, they might pop out altogether. While this is certainly not the case, a more plausible-sounding idea suggests that the eyelids close to protect your eyes from the multitude of germs you're expelling into the immediate environment. However, neither theory holds much sway among the medical community.

In fact, the reason we blink is a simple reflex reaction, as natural as closing your eyes when something gets too close to your face. The nose and eyes are linked via shared cranial nerves – so when the brain sends a command telling the nose to 'let rip', another signal automatically goes to the eyelids telling them to blink.

Despite this, some individuals have been able to train themselves to sneeze with their eyes open. Many of them learn to do this only by repeatedly physically propping their eyelids open at the vital moment. One can only assume that they consider this a good use of their time and effort – but most of us can't help wondering why bother? Surely it can't be that exciting to watch your own nasal evacuations?

57 Contact the dead

WHAT IT IS Communicating with the 'other side'
WHY YOU WON'T DO IT Dead men tend not to tell tales

There's nothing more painful than losing a loved one, especially if we have not had the chance to say our farewells, so it's no wonder many people are fascinated with the possibility of contact beyond the grave. Science says it is impossible and that those who claim to do it are frauds, but more people than ever retain the faith.

Spiritualism, the belief in a spirit world with open communication channels to the living, gained popularity in the mid-19th century, reaching its peak after the trauma of the First World War. From the earliest days of the movement, it lacked credibility among the scientific community, but rarely wanted for high-profile and respected advocates, perhaps the most famous of whom was the Sherlock Holmes author Sir Arthur Conan Doyle. Spiritualism is a faith movement, and believers accuse sceptics of a failure of faith.

Perhaps the most well-known spiritualist figure is the medium, an individual who claims to be able to communicate between the living and the dead. While there are distinct variations in the way that mediums claim to work, there are two broad schools. In the first, the medium maintains their own personality throughout, and 'speaks' with the dead (often ostensibly with the help of a 'spirit guide') before communicating relevant messages to the living. In the second school, the medium goes into a trance-like state and 'channels' the spirit, perhaps adopting alien forms of speech and even appearance.

Much criticism is levelled at mediums, not least that they take financial and emotional advantage of vulnerable, even gullible, people who have suffered great loss. There are also regular accusations that the effects of mediumship are achieved fraudulently, through practices such as 'cold and hot reading. Cold reading is the deduction of information by picking up on, for instance, physical appearance, body language, vocal ticks and asides: the spiritualist then claims this information was passed to them from the spirit world. Hot reading aims at a similar effect, but in this case the information is acquired by, for instance, actively researching a client or audience member before an appointment or show.

Some spiritualists prefer the seance, a gathering of believers who attempt to use their combined energies to invoke the spirits. A gathering of three or its multiples is sometimes recommended,

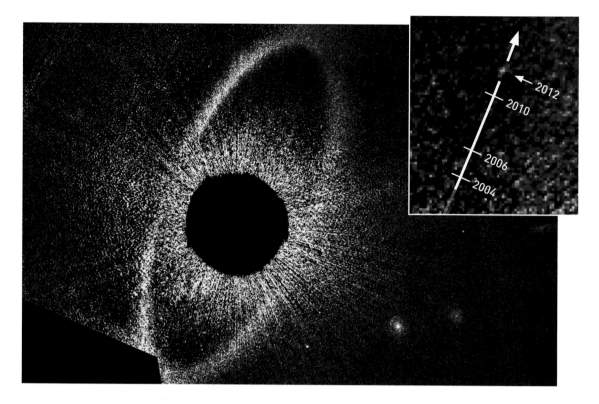

DEEP SPACE *This Hubble Space Telescope image shows the star Fomalhaut surrounded by a disc of planet-forming gas and dust. The sharp inner edge of this ring is thought to be created by the gravity of an unseen planet. The inset tracks the motion of a second suspected planet moving through the disc between 2004 and 2010.*

planet orbits a star, the velocity of the star's orbit around the system's centre of mass will vary slightly. Astronomers can detect this by analysing the spectrum of starlight. By interpreting changes known as Doppler shifts, they can work out the mass and orbit of any large planets.

• Astrometry. This technique relies on detecting slight motions in stars caused by orbiting planets. In effect, astronomers are looking for stars that have a visible 'wobble' in the sky.

• Transits. In this method, the astronomer uses special equipment to detect a fractional and periodic dimming of a star's brightness, caused when a planet passes between the star and the observer and blocks out the star's light.

• Gravitational microlensing. A technique that utilizes Einstein's theory of relativity. When a planet passes in front of a star, its gravity acts as a lens to focus light rays from the star, leading to a temporary increase in the star's brightness and making it seem like it has moved slightly.

• Polarimetry. A method using the fact that starlight oscillates in a particular direction when it bounces off a planet and through the planet's atmosphere. These rays are said to be 'polarized', while rays are normally 'unpolarized' (i.e. they oscillate in random directions).

If that all sounds like too much hard work, you can help find a planet from the comfort of your own home, as long as you have a computer. In 2010 researchers from some of the world's finest universities launched planethunters.org, an automatic transit-searching system to which you can contribute.

59 Practise telepathy

Telepathy is the act of communicating thoughts or ideas by means beyond the known senses. Most of the scientific community dismisses the notion as hokum, but there are others who remain convinced that it exists. So how can you best establish whether you might have the gift?

The term 'telepathy' was coined by poet and psychical researcher Frederic Myers in the late Victorian period – a time when there was a burgeoning interest in the paranormal. Most who claim the gift state that it demands faith. If you don't believe that telepathy exists, they say, then you will not be able to develop your skills. In other words, sceptics need not apply.

Here is a basic experiment from the 'thought transference' canon. Since telepathy requires more than one participant, find an open-minded friend or two who are willing to embark on the project with you.

Prepare a series of flash cards – seven to ten is a good number to start with. On each card write a single, simple word or draw a picture. Don't choose anything too complicated or abstract at this stage: 'cat' or 'house' will work better than 'carburettor' or 'panini'.

Go with your partner somewhere quiet and devoid of distractions. Sit opposite each other, adopting relaxed poses.

Decide which of you is the 'sender' and which the 'receiver'. The sender should try to clear their mind of any extraneous thoughts and worries. A blank mind, so the theory goes, is a more receptive one.

The sender picks a card at random and focuses intently on the image, repeating it silently in their mind for half a minute or so. The receiver, eyes closed, tries to pick up the message from the sender. When they think they have it, they should say the word and note down if they were correct or not. Some artistic people may prefer to form a picture in their heads and then attempt to draw it on a sketch pad.

After a few minutes, sender and receiver can swap roles and repeat the experiment. You may wish to move on to using playing cards or choosing random words and images from a magazine. If your results are spectacular, you must decide for yourself whether you think there is something telepathic going on, whether you're picking up or sending subconscious cues, or if you might simply be a lucky guesser.

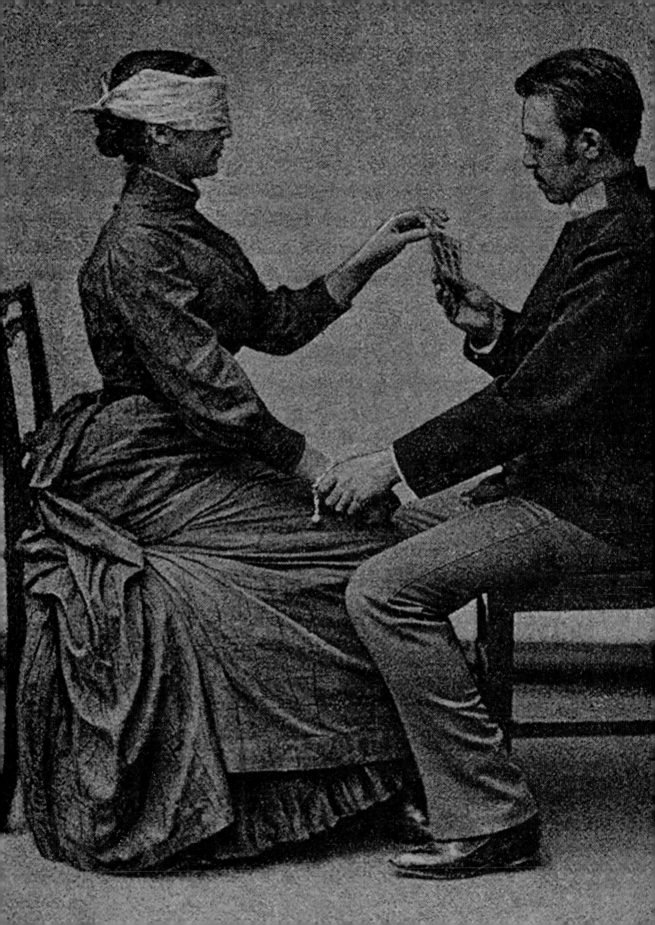

60 Meet a dodo

WHAT IT IS A long-lost resident of Mauritius
WHY YOU WON'T DO IT We don't have the phrase 'dead as a dodo' for no reason

An ungainly relative of the pigeon, the dodo has long been the 'poster bird' for all species threatened by extinction, though it might have been forgotten altogether were it not for a celebrated appearance in *Alice's Adventures in Wonderland*. If you want to see one today, then head for Oxford and prepare to compromise!

The dodo (scientific name *Raphus cucullatus*) lived happily for millions of years on the Indian Ocean island paradise of Mauritius. Its ancestors probably flew here shortly after the islands formed in volcanic eruptions about 10 million years ago, but evolved their way to flightlessness as they settled into the easy life in their predator-free tropical paradise. With no need to worry about getting off the ground, adults could grow to 90 centimetres (3 ft) long and weigh up to 20 kilograms (44 lb). They had grey plumage and small residual wings, and feasted on a diet of fruits and seeds that littered the forest floors.

All that changed when hungry Dutch sailors landed on the island in 1598. The birds became an immediate target, and they were widely hunted, despite their meat being tough and unappealing. It was because of this that they were named '*walckvogel*' or 'disgusting bird' – talk about adding insult to injury! As well as hunting the dodo, humans introduced a host of predators (either on the birds themselves, or on their vulnerable eggs),

such as pigs, rats, dogs and cats. They also degraded the dodo's habitat, and within 80 years the last dodo was dead. So effective was the annihilation that not a single preserved bird, nor even a complete skeleton has come down to us. A few museums, notably in Dublin and Oxford, do boast dodo skeletons but they are composed of bones from several different creatures.

In 2007, the most complete skeleton ever found was discovered in a cave on Mauritius – it may yet yield dodo DNA. Until then, the most complete remains containing soft tissue are to be found at Oxford University's Museum of Natural History. The stuffed specimen displayed here was originally in naturalist John Tradescant's London museum, but had suffered severe decay by the mid-18th century. Today only the bird's head and one of its feet remain in a mummified form, but they were still enough to inspire Oxford mathematician Charles Dodgson, better known as Lewis Carroll, to include the dodo among the inhabitants of his famous Wonderland.

The Dodo.

Geo Edwards, Sculp: A.D. 1757

61 Find two identical snowflakes

WHAT IT IS The climatic equivalent of finding a needle in a haystack
WHY YOU WON'T DO IT You'll struggle even to preserve two flakes long enough to inspect them

Can there be anything more romantic than staring out at a world shrouded in white on a winter's day, safe in the knowledge that no two snowflakes are the same? We owe the idea that no two flakes are the same to one Wilson Bentley, the amateur scientist who around 1885 developed the first process for photographing snowflakes in detail.

Wilson Bentley reached his remarkable conclusion from careful study of more than 5,000 snowflake images over several years – but how does it stand up to modern science? Snow forms when humid air rich in water vapour is cooled to very low temperatures. The vapour condenses to form ice crystals around tiny nuclei such as specks of dust, and grows rapidly, developing one of a handful of basic structures, all with an essentially hexagonal plan thanks to the pattern in which water molecules bond to each other.

The exact shape depends on several factors, including temperature range, air currents, speed of descent through the air, humidity and proximity to other snowflakes. Flakes may rise and fall through an 'air column' several times, changing form as they go, before they are eventually heavy enough to fall to the ground. Impurities in the water droplets also have an effect on the overall structure. So the odds of a snowflake making it to the ground without imperfections and asymmetric oddities

are limited. And the chances of randomly finding two flakes of exactly the same shape and size are thus exceedingly low. However, in 1988, Nancy Knight of the National Center for Atmospheric Research in Colorado, discovered two 'identical' flakes under her microscope. The crystals came from a research plane that had collected them in mid-air on a chilled slide – perhaps Bentley was wrong, after all?

But then again, it depends if you're looking at the molecular level. Consider the numbers involved – even the most humble snowflake will contain around 10^{18} water molecules. Around one in every 500 of these will contain a heavy 'isotope' of oxygen – an ^{18}O atom rather than the standard ^{16}O atom. So even that small flake will contain some 10^{16} of these variant molecules. To assume that any two flakes would have these 'rogue' molecules positioned identically in their structures pushes the realms of probability. And even if there ever have been two such flakes, the chances of proving it are negligible.

62 Hunt a ghost

WHAT IT IS Tracking the
spirits of the dead
WHY YOU WON'T DO IT
No one has yet proven
that ghosts exist

Ghosts – the spirits of the dead – may or may not exist. But it is certain that we remain fascinated by the idea that the souls of the departed have not departed as completely as they should have. If you're not sufficiently spooked by a horror movie or a trip on the ghost train at the fairground, you can always start hunting spirits. But be warned, you might just find one...

Ghosts seem to have little place in our rational world – yet a survey carried out in 2008 revealed that 34 per cent of Americans believe in their existence. As with all investigations into the paranormal, however, it pays to be sceptical: if something seems odd, don't jump to far-out conclusions, but search for a scientific explanation.

If science can't provide an answer to a question, then you can start speculating about whether there really are, to paraphrase Shakespeare, more things in heaven and earth than are dreamt of in our philosophy.

Those who believe in ghosts argue that there are numerous indicators that a spirit may be present. They include:
• Apparitions (spotting Anne Boleyn floating down a corridor with her head under her arm would be a good hint that ghosts do exist after all).
• Inexplicable noises.
• Strange smells.
• 'Cold spots', where the temperature in a room suddenly drops.

• Signs of agitation among animals.
• Objects that have mysteriously moved (objects moving of their own accord in front of you might suggest the presence of a poltergeist).

When planning a ghost hunt, select a potential haunted location for yourself and ensure you have the necessary permission for access. Assuming ghosts exist, they can presumably haunt any location, but places with long and tragic pasts seem to generate most sightings. Examples include the Tower of London, with its history of brutal executions and torture, and the Myrtles Plantation in Louisiana, with its stories of slavery and murder.

Do your research thoroughly. Investigate the history of your chosen location, reading books or going through newspaper archives. Speak to any residents, patients or employees associated with your chosen site, either currently or in the past. Try to work out who might be haunting there and why.

GHOST HUNTERS *Two members of the Valley Rangers Paranormal Investigators, Daniel Bidondi and Mike Welliver, attempt to entice the ghosts said to inhabit the Cumberland Monastery on Rhode Island to show themselves in 2005.*

Arm yourself with equipment to gather evidence. A ghost hunter's typical kit might include:
• Night vision goggles – the favoured ghost-hunting hours are from midnight until four in the morning, when it is far too dark to see much with the naked eye.
• Still and video cameras – even when a ghost hunter has not seen anything unusual at the moment of taking a photo or recording, they may find unexpected features (such as glowing 'orbs') when reviewing the images.
• An electromagnetic field (EMF) meter – to track unusual electromagnetic fluctuations.
• A dowsing rod, often in the form of a forked branch; believers argue these can reveal changes in

unspecified 'energy fields'.
• A digital thermometer – to help confirm the presence of 'cold spots'.
• An audio recorder – to capture any other-worldly noises.
• Infrared sensors – to track unexplained movements in a room.

Many sceptics challenge the validity of such evidence-gathering, since it is inevitably done in an uncontrolled environment. In addition, there are scientific explanations for most if not all commonly reported phenomena. Cold spots, for instance, can often be explained by natural environmental factors, while photographic anomalies are usually a result of tricks of the light, or errant dust or water particles. Nonetheless, if you do believe that you've witnessed a haunting, the more evidence you can offer the better. This, along with general safety, is another good reason to do your ghost hunting in company.

Time travel

WHAT IT IS A distortion of
the linear nature of time
WHY YOU WON'T DO IT
See *Back to the Future* for
what can go wrong

Aside from belligerent Martians, nothing has occupied the minds
of science fiction writers as much as the possibility of time travel.
So if you fancy reliving the past, seeing your future or popping
back in time to meet your great-grandfather, how realistic
are your chances?

In some ways, we're all time travellers
already – a second ago we were in the
past, now we're in the present and we'll
shortly be in the future. Okay, that's
cheating – what we really mean by
time travel is journeying into the future
more quickly than we do normally, or
rewinding time and travelling to the past.

Accelerated travel into the future, at
least, has a strong scientific basis.
Albert Einstein's famous theory of

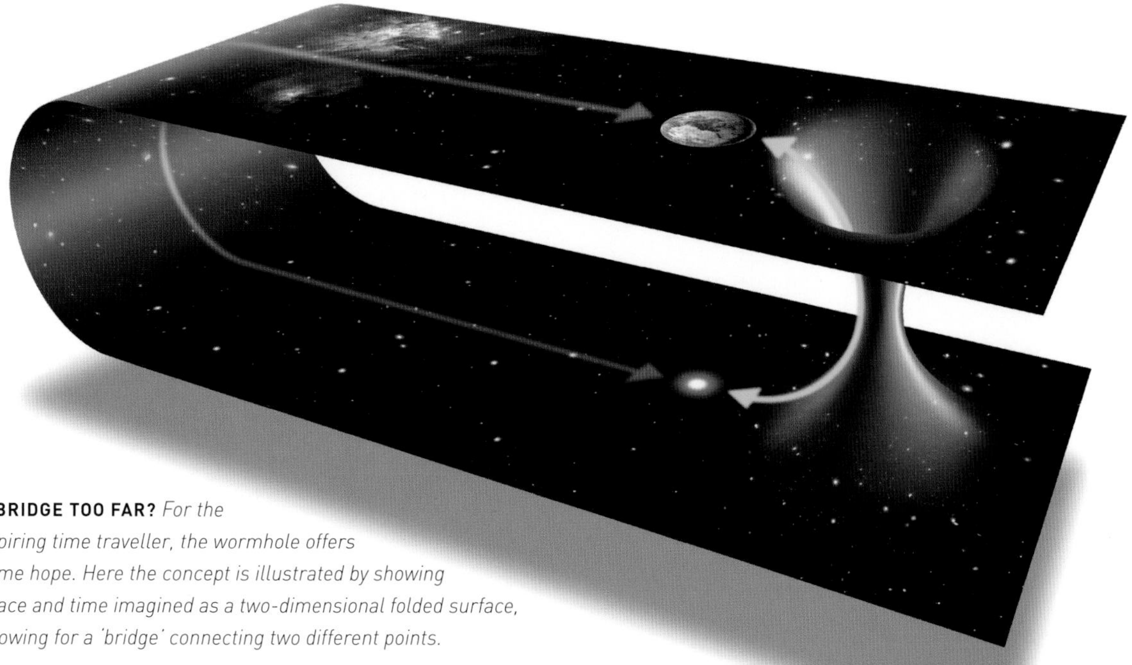

A BRIDGE TOO FAR? *For the
aspiring time traveller, the wormhole offers
some hope. Here the concept is illustrated by showing
space and time imagined as a two-dimensional folded surface,
allowing for a 'bridge' connecting two different points.*

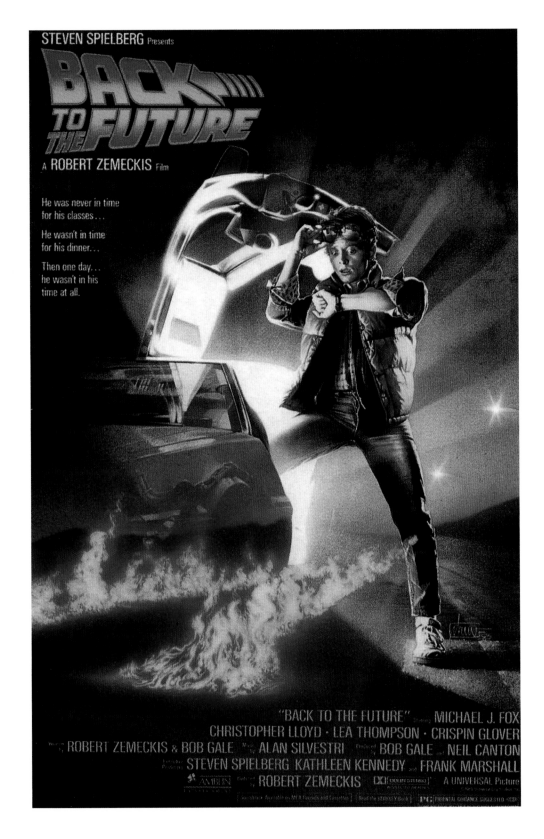

general relativity shows how time is affected by the gravity of large masses, moving at different speeds in different locations. This effect is called gravitational time dilation, and it's been proved in many ways – for instance, the clocks of GPS satellites orbiting high above Earth pick up about a third of a billionth of a second per day over time compared to their ground-based equivalents.

Obviously this is not something we would normally notice, but if we were able to, say, travel close to a huge black hole, such as Sagittarius A at the centre of our galaxy, we would experience time at half the speed of Earth. If we left Earth at the beginning of the year and spent a year circling the back hole, then by the time we returned home, two years would have passed on Earth. We would have travelled forwards in time.

Another form of time dilation effect happens when objects move at speeds close to the speed of light. Get close enough to the Universe's ultimate speed limit, and you could travel for a week and miss a century of life on Earth. But to achieve this, you would need a vehicle 2,000 times faster than the fastest manned spacecraft ever built.

Confused yet? Well, we haven't even started on travelling backwards in time. Our greatest minds are much less certain this is possible even in theory, but if it is, then some believe the answer again rests with black holes. Specifically, a 'Kerr black hole' is a theoretical construct created by rings of superdense neutron stars behaving in particular ways. This black hole could suck you in at one point and expel you at another, possibly in the future but perhaps in the past.

A slightly more familiar concept is the wormhole. This is a hypothetical tunnel through space and time connecting distant parts of the Universe. Scientists believe that wormholes exist in the submicroscopic 'quantum foam' of the Universe – but their entrance tunnels are less than a billion-billion-trillionth of a centimetre across. It's clearly going to take more than a diet and some lycra to squeeze into that kind of opening, but some scientists believe that it might one day be possible to construct a giant version.

Elsewhere, physicist J. Richard Gott has outlined his theory of cosmic strings, objects that are narrower than an atom but exert massive gravitational pull affecting time dilation. By bringing two strings close together, it might be possible to form a time loop, propelling you into the future or back into the past.

If backward time travel is possible, however, many theorists are convinced that it would not be possible to go back further than the moment at which the method of travel was invented. This might explain why up we are not currently inundated with visitors from the future.

Of course, if it turns out that we can go back in time, we'll still need to iron out causality. If one thing happens as a result of another, what happens if we go back and change the initial event? That's the question posed by the 'grandfather paradox' – if you decide to go back in time to kill your grandfather when he is a child, your father won't be born. And if he isn't born, neither are you. So how can you be around to travel back through time in the first place? For more of this sort of thing, treat yourself to a box set of the *Back to the Future* movies.

64 Spontaneously combust

In 2011, a 76-year-old man was discovered lying face down near the fireplace in the living room of his home in Galway, Ireland. An inquest declared that he had died of spontaneous combustion, a phenomenon many scientists believe does not exist. It is not something that you want to try, but how might it happen to you?

According to believers, spontaneous human combustion (SHC) involves a person bursting into flames despite the apparent absence of an external heat source. In most reported cases, the body of the victim is charred, while the immediate environment around the body is unharmed.

The earliest known account dates to 1663, when Danish anatomist Thomas Bartholin described how a Parisian woman had gone up in smoke while she slept, leaving her straw bed intact. Perhaps the most famous case, however, is a fictional one – the death of the rag-and-bottle merchant Krook in Charles Dickens's *Bleak House* (published 1853).

Estimates suggest that up to 200,000 reported cases of SHC have accumulated over the past few centuries, but the vast majority have not been subject to proper scientific investigation, and investigators continue to spar about possible causes.

Few people give credence to extremist explanations such as the idea that

spontaneous combustion is some sort of divine intervention. Similarly, obvious scientific solutions – for instance, that all incidents can be attributed to flammable nightwear – have been ruled out.

One oft-cited theory is the so-called 'wick effect', in which a person's own body fat fuels a slow smouldering combustion. Any fire requires both fuel and sufficient heat to ignite it, and a sizeable number of cases have indeed involved overweight people with large amounts of body fat to burn, but there have also been plenty of apparent victims on the skinny side.

But the wick effect is not actually reliant on excessive quantities of body fat. It simply requires a regular source of ignition, such as a cigarette to set fire to the victim's clothing. If their skin splits to expose body fat, the victim becomes a 'human candle', with their clothing acting as a wick and the fat as candle wax. The 'wick' slowly burns until the fat is used up, but leaves the surrounding area unscathed. This effect, however, does not seem to account for victims whose skin is charred but whose internal organs remain intact – and this last point also mitigates against the idea that SHC occurs when enzymes ignite flammable methane gas in the intestines.

Some have put forward the idea that a build-up of static electricity can cause the clothing and person inside to ignite (and indeed there have been few reported incidences of naked SHC victims). Others have suggested that electric fields within the body can short-circuit somehow, causing an internal electrical fire. Another popular theory involves blood alcohol levels increasing to the point of flammability – Krook in *Bleak House*, for instance, is a heavy drinker. The idea that even the most alcoholic blood could ignite spontaneously is regarded with scepticism by the scientific community, but add a lit cigarette to the equation...

Perhaps a more rational explanation is that spontaneous combustion is an illusion that requires a rare, but not impossible, coincidence of circumstances. An external source, such as a lit cigarette or an ember, provides the heat to ignite flammable material, such as clothing. The victim is unable to escape the fire source or put themselves out, and their clothes act as a wick. Their body fat then fuels the fire, but they are sufficiently isolated from their surroundings to prevent other objects from igniting. Finally, the creation of insulating ash puts the fire out once all the body fat has burned away.

BURNING QUESTION *The eerie image of one Ms E.M., whose 69-year-old body was discovered in West London in January 1958. Her body reduced to ash, the official cause of death was given as 'preternatural combustability'.*

Be struck by lightning twice

According to popular folklore, lightning never strikes the same place twice. But comforting though that thought may be, it's far from the truth – multiple strikes happen all too regularly. Of course, there's no good reason you'd want to be struck by lightning even once, let alone twice – but here's how it could happen.

In 2003, a scientific study funded by NASA at the University of Arizona identified the locations of almost 400 lightning strikes, and revealed that about one-third of all strikes hit two or more spots close to each other. A number of these generated third and even fourth lightning strokes, but these were most likely to follow the paths of one of the first two strokes. All of this goes to show that it is quite possible to be struck by lightning twice by a single bolt.

Lightning is still poorly understood, but seems to be triggered when a strong electrical field builds up between negative charges at the bottom of a storm cloud and positive charges on the ground. A lightning strike is thus an attempt by nature to restore the circuit. It leaves a trail of charged or 'ionized' air in its wake, opening up a path for further strikes.

If an object is struck once, it is no less likely to be struck again, and tall, exposed points are obviously vulnerable. The Empire State Building, for instance, can count on being struck between 25 and 100 times each year.

In any one year, you have about a 1 in 700,000 chance of being struck by lightning. Fatalities stand at about 10 per cent, and usually result from the electric current stopping the heart or compromising other major organs. Survivors are likely to suffer burns and stroke-like effects.

You're most likely to fall victim to a strike if you remain outside during a thunderstorm. Putting yourself next to a tall object, such as a tree or pylon, radically increases your risk, as does holding aloft an umbrella, flying a kite or waving golf clubs around. One man who was living evidence of lightning striking the same spot more than once was Roy Sullivan, a park ranger from Virginia who was first struck in 1942. A 27-year hiatus ensued before a further six strikes from 1969 to 1977. He also told of a further hit in his childhood though this incident could not be verified.

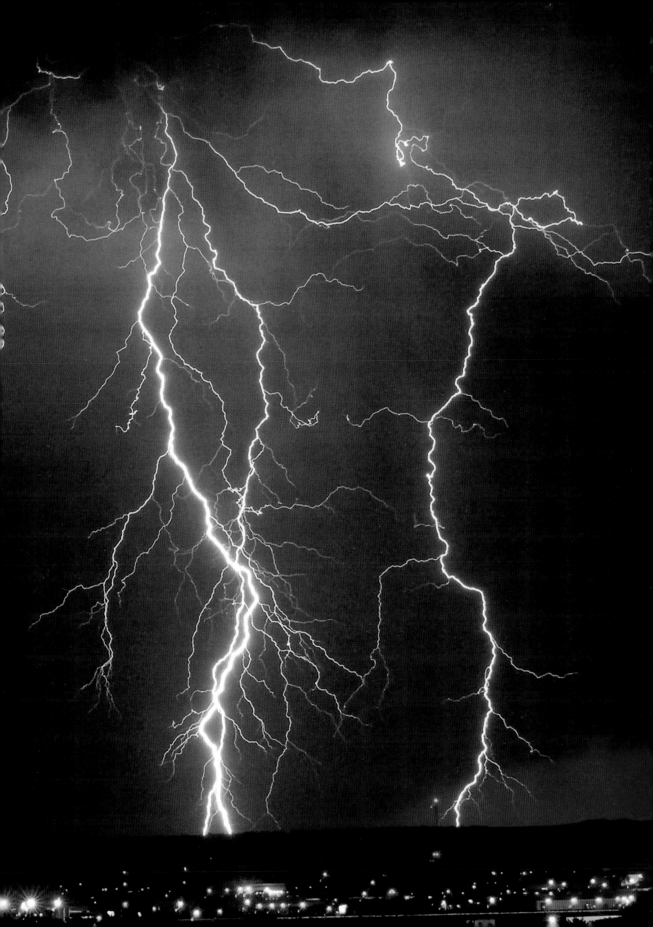

66 | See a UFO

WHAT IT IS Spotting our alien cousins zipping around in the sky
WHY YOU WON'T DO IT Those little green men are nothing if not discreet

Are you one of those people who think *E.T.* and *The X-Files* are documentaries? Are you sure we are not alone and that little green men in flying saucers are constantly whizzing about our skies? If so, then no doubt you'd love to see a UFO for yourself – but what do you need to know when going out to look for aliens?

Strictly speaking, the term 'UFO' means Unidentified Flying Object. Just because you don't immediately recognize an object doesn't mean it's automatically a flying saucer manned by a crew of little green men who want you to take them to your leader, and in fact the vast majority of UFO reports turn out to have fairly mundane explanations.

Concrete data about UFO sightings is understandably hard to accumulate and verify – reports are anecdotal by their very nature, and while some people are only too happy to trumpet their 'close encounters', others are far more sheepish about putting their reputations as level-headed individuals on the line. However, some estimates suggest around 80–95 per cent of all reported sightings can be explained in one way or another, leaving an obstinate core of 5–20 per cent that remain genuinely unidentified.

So if you think you might have spotted a UFO, try to employ a scientific and rational approach. Consider whether it might actually be one of the following and start by ruling out what it *isn't*:

• An astronomical object such as a planet, moon or star. Venus, in particular, is often mistaken for something less familiar. If you see a bright light in the same place in the sky night after night, might it simply be a star? Purchase a star chart for quick reference.

• A 'normal' space phenomenon, such as an asteroid hurtling through the sky. Earth regularly passes through streams of shooting stars, and if a particularly large asteroid comes through our orbit, it will often make the news.

• A human aircraft. Technology is developing all the time and it's worth considering whether you might have caught a glimpse of an experimental aeroplane design or a human spacecraft re-entering the atmosphere. It might even be just a satellite. NASA and other websites publish timetables of when certain bright satellites (such as the International Space Station and the Iridium communication satellites) will be visible at particular locations, so check their records for a potential explanation.

are seeing things in the sky that are not really there. Certain extreme examples are known as Fata Morgana and can lead to distinctly earth-bound objects being transformed into unrecognizable forms in the sky. Moon dogs, meanwhile, are bright spots of light created by ice crystals refracting moonlight.

• You must also be aware of the dangers from a deliberate hoax. There's money and fame to be made from tales of UFOs, and plenty of people are prepared to manufacture them. Consider, for instance, the 1980 Rendlesham Forest incident. Staff at a US Air Force base in eastern England, reported a string of unexplained lights, but in 2003 a security policeman claimed that they actually came from his Plymouth Volaré and were part of an elaborate practical joke.

If you are convinced that your UFO is none of the above, try to gather evidence. Reach for a camera or a tape recorder – or at the very least, make some notes and sketches. You might want to inform the authorities, but be prepared for them not to take you seriously.

ALIEN INVASION? *Signs warn trespassers from straying into Nevada's Area 51. A military base that implements high levels of secrecy, it has long been touted as the storage location of a crashed spacecraft allegedly recovered from Roswell, New Mexico, in 1947.*

• A weather balloon. These useful meteorological tools have caused a good deal of confusion among UFO-spotters over the years, and can even trigger reports when they fall to Earth.
• A flare, a firework or a searchlight, all of which have explained many mysterious light flashes.
• Animal activity. Be prepared for your Martian landing craft to be a small group of migrating pigeons, or a flock of geese illuminated from below.
• Natural light phenomena. Mirages are caused when light rays are bent in such a way as to make us believe we

If you are actively seeking out UFOs, where are the best places to look? Many ufologists see Roswell, New Mexico, and the US Air Force's 'Area 51' in Nevada as their spiritual homes. Los Angeles is the city with most reported sightings, but what else would you expect from the home of the entertainment business? And what about Bonnybridge in Scotland? There have reportedly been more than 300 sightings annually in a town of 6,000, although sceptics point out that these reports have done no harm to local tourism.

In all your dealings, be prepared to accept the most logical explanation – even if it's not the most exciting. Stay rational if you want to avoid accusations of being a crank.

Solve the Millennium Prize Problems

WHAT IT IS A series of the most perplexing maths conundrums imaginable
WHY YOU WON'T DO IT Because adding two and two together doesn't always equal four

In 2000 the Clay Mathematics Institute in Providence, Rhode Island, issued a list of seven seriously brain-boggling mathematical problems. If you're one of those people who used to enjoy doing your daily Sudoku but can now finish even the really hard ones in a couple of minutes, then the Millennium Prize Problems could be that new challenge you've been looking for.

Proving the veracity (or not) of any of the seven selected theories has implications not only for mathematicians but for practitioners in disciplines as diverse as aeronautics, medicine, philosophy, computing and theoretical physics. Best of all, if you have the vision to solve any single one of them, you will qualify for a million-dollar prize.

First of all, choose which problem you are going to tackle. (Thinking you'll solve more than one is probably unrealistic.) At present, only one of the Millennium Problems has been resolved. The other six are so complex that even explaining them fully would need a book in itself.
• The Riemann Hypothesis. Bernhard Riemann's 1859 formula describes the distribution of prime numbers, but can anyone prove that it's true for *all possible* numbers?
• The Hodge Conjecture deals with the grey area where algebra and geometry converge, but in a way far beyond the imagination of most of us 'ordinary Joes'.
• The Birch and Swinnerton-Dyer Conjecture is a heady mix of rational numbers, elliptic curves and unsolved formulae.
• And those are the relatively simpler ones to grasp...Two that are definitely not for the beginner are the Yang-Mills existence and mass gap (with profound implications for our understanding of quantum physics) and the Navier-Stokes Theorem, a series of 19th-century equations dealing with fluid motion.
• Finally comes 'P versus NP' – a sort of meta-problem concerned with theories of problem-solving themselves.

The seventh, now-resolved problem was the Poincaré Conjecture (concerning shapes that exist in four or more dimensions). In 2010 the Clay Institute announced that Russian mathematician Grigori Perelman had qualified for a prize for his solution to the problem. However, Perelman then turned down his reward, reportedly on the grounds that he believed it should have been shared with Richard Hamilton, whose theories he had drawn upon. Obviously for some people, money isn't everything.

Practise telekinesis

Telekinesis – a term coined by Russian author Alexander Aksakov in 1890 – is the alleged ability to harness the power of the human mind to move distant objects. There's precious little scientific proof that it exists, but that has not stopped the world's superpowers investigating. So how could it be done?

Telekinesis is a branch of psychokinesis, the ability to influence the physical world with the power of the mind alone. In a 2006 US survey, around 30 per cent of respondents indicated they believed the idea to be plausible – but there has never been a single controlled laboratory experiment to prove it. Despite this, it's widely acknowledged that during the Cold War, both the US and Soviet governments were actively involved in telekinetic and psychokinetic research. The Americans, for instance, reputedly ran Project Jedi, which aimed to create a breed of 'super-soldier' able to kill by thought alone.

This project is detailed in the book and film *The Men Who Stare at Goats* – a title that refers to a series of experiments at Fort Bragg, North Carolina, in which potential psychics tried to kill goats simply by focusing their thoughts. Uri Geller, perhaps the world's foremost claimant of psychokinetic abilities (shown opposite), says that he was asked to take part, but as an animal-lover, he declined and stuck to bending spoons.

Most advocates of telekinesis suggest that to develop your own abilities, you must have faith in your potential. The required skills, they say, take a long time to perfect. Start by meditating, relaxing yourself entirely and clearing your mind. Practise breathing exercises and consider chanting mantras. Then gradually begin to build up periods of intense concentration. (Until, say, you can focus on a particular thought or emotion to the exclusion of everything else for 15 minutes at a time.)

Do not start out with big ambitions – even believers would say it's highly unlikely that you'll be able to move stationary objects at once. Instead, try to prolong the momentum of an already moving object, such as a spinning coin. Progress to trying to move small objects, such as matchsticks sealed off from air currents under a bell jar. If you show signs of success, be careful who you tell about your newfound talent – do you really want to answer the door one day to a soldier or CIA operative, complete with accompanying goat?

69 Firewalk

Firewalking is an ancient rite, practised in India at least by 1200 BC. There are long traditions throughout Asia, Africa and the Pacific Islands, usually associated with religious or coming-of-age ceremonies. Heating fuel to very high temperatures and then walking across it does not sound like a sensible pastime – but if you approach this challenge in the right way, you can emerge entirely unscathed.

According to many of its practitioners, firewalking proves the concept of 'mind over matter', where an individual uses their mental and psychological capacities to overcome physical impediments. But in fact, despite appearances, science is firmly on the side of the firewalker. If you are tempted to give it a go, contact an organized group who will ensure you are fully prepared and at the least risk possible of injury. You will be encouraged to relax your mind and relieve your body of any tension before embarking upon your walk. You may be led in deep breathing exercises and asked to meditate. Regardless of whether you believe in any faith-based aspects of these routines, ensuring that you are well and truly relaxed will only increase your chances of success.

The coals upon which you walk are likely to be around 550°C (1,020°F) – more than enough to burn your soles to a cinder over a typical walk of 3–4 metres (10–13 ft), you might think. However, heat is transferred in this case by conduction from one medium to another – and efficient conduction relies on each material being a good conductor of heat. This is where nature lends the firewalker a helping hand: coal that has been burning for a long time develops a lightweight structure that is not brilliantly suited to conduction. In addition, a substantial coating of ash forms and acts as insulation.

Similarly, your feet are not the best conductors, so to avoid burning, the trick is simply to make sure that your feet and the coals are not in contact long enough to establish efficient conduction. This is why firewalkers tend to adopt a brisk stride. But do not be tempted to run – your increased momentum will force your feet deep down into the coals, putting them at greater risk.

Before you start your walk, be sure that the bed of coals has been checked for any foreign objects that might act as good conductors, such as metal items, and as soon as you've finished, dip your toes in cold water and give yourself a well-deserved pat on the back.

70 Become invisible

WHAT IT IS Disappearing
into the background
WHY YOU WON'T DO IT
The science is lagging
far behind the idea

In the absence of a Harry Potter-style cloak of invisibility, making yourself disappear seems like a tall order. Fortunately, however, some of our brightest thinkers have been coming up with alternative methods, some of which seem just as magical. Using technology instead of magic or superpowers might seem like a cheat, but if the end result is the same, does it really matter?

When we see an object, what we are actually seeing is light rays bouncing off the object and into our eyes. If something allows light to pass through it without absorbing or reflecting any of it, the object becomes invisible to the viewer. While there are certain natural materials that are transparent to a lesser or greater degree, none is 100 per cent – so developing more transparent materials is one aspect of the invisibility challenge faced by researchers, while finding ways to conceal non-transparent objects within them is a second, even more difficult problem.

The defence industry has long had an interest in developing technology that allows objects (from personnel to aircraft, tanks and submarines) to move around without being detected by radar. This has given rise to stealth technology, also known as 'low observable technology'. In some respects, this is the closest we have yet come to achieving invisibility – though a stealth bomber, for instance, may still be very obviously visible to the human eye

even if it goes undetected by radar. (The bombers are painted in dark colours and usually operate at night to ameliorate this problem.)

A radar-detecting system relies on being able to detect radar waves being reflected off an object. A stealth bomber's invisibility to radar is thus achieved by several means, including:
• A distinct shape that redirects the electromagnetic waves from radars.
• Metal plates that reduce reflection of radar waves.
• A 'skin' that absorbs radar waves, bouncing them around internally until the waves lose their energy.
• Special radar-absorbent paints that convert radar rays into heat.

In the same way that stealth technology aims to stop reflection of radar waves, those looking to develop invisibility to the human eye seek to prevent objects from reflecting light rays. This has led to the development of new 'metamaterials' – materials that have been engineered to have properties not seen in nature.

172   SCIENCE AND THE NATURAL WORLD

HIDE AND SEEK *The B-2 Spirit (or stealth bomber) is built by Northrop Grumman and was introduced into service in 1997. With a unit cost of approximately three-quarters of a billion US dollars, invisibility does not come cheap.*

A team at the University of California, Berkeley, has created a fishnet-style material by stacking together silver and metal dielectric layers and then perforating them with holes. This material refracts light negatively to make things appear where they are not. For instance, a fish in a stream might appear to float above the water's surface. Meanwhile, another team at the same university created a metamaterial that sends light around an object, much as water passes round a rock in a river. By bending the light rays round an object, the rays are not reflected off it, thus rendering it invisible.

Both of these developments take us considerably closer to the point where we really may be able to call upon invisibility cloaks. However, the technology remains in its infancy and while they prove that light can be 'bent the wrong way' to fool the eye, it will be a good while before we will be able to effectively hide objects of any great size. As Jason Valentine, one of the Berkeley researchers, has admitted: 'I don't think we have to worry about invisible people walking round anytime soon.'

Indeed, perhaps that is something we should be grateful for. While invisibility cloaks can't come soon enough for military personnel who wish to slip in and out of conflict zones unseen, think of the implications in the wider world: fare-dodgers sneaking onto buses and trains without paying; rogues left to commit their crimes in the knowledge that no witness will be able to supply a photofit; embittered ex-paramours secretly joining you as you re-enter the dating scene. And as or nudist beaches, it hardly bears thinking about!

71

Live forever

WHAT IT IS Supping from the cup of immortality
WHY YOU WON'T DO IT There are only two certainties in this life: death and taxes

'Who wants to live forever?' asked the rock band Queen in one of their hits. Quite a lot of us it seems – judging by the amount of time, energy and money thrown at stretching our lifespans ever further. And when it comes to longevity, the human race is definitely heading in the right direction.

In the days of the Roman Empire, life expectancy was a depressingly low 28 years, while today the global average sits at just over 67 years (with dramatic regional variations). But that is still a long way short of 'forever'. The trouble is, we humans are hardwired to reproduce ourselves. For all the great achievements of humanity, like any other animal this is our primary function. And alas for us, we're built to do this relatively early in our lives and, after that begin to wear down until we eventually die.

We can increase our chances of long life by looking after ourselves and avoiding all those foolish pastimes like drinking too much alcohol, smoking and eating too many cream cakes. But experts agree that even in conquering these health challenges, we cannot protect ourselves from unforeseeable dramatic events. We could still be cut off in our prime, just before our 12,000th birthday, by a speeding bus or massive meteorite.

However, some scientists believe that there are children alive today who might yet live to be 1,000. This would rely on several medical breakthroughs: in order to preserve life *ad infinitum*, we need to be able to replace lost cells, keep them clean of debris, avoid damaging mutations, stop cancerous multiplications and prevent 'extracellular protein crosslinks' that cause issues such as hardened arteries. New innovations such as stem cell technology increase the probability of us eventually being able to meet all these challenges. A further theory goes that the more we know, the quicker we'll know more. That is to say, the rate of breakthroughs (such as cures for cancer) may accelerate exponentially.

Sadly, the chances of the necessary discoveries coming within our own lifetimes remain remote. Fortunately, there are other options, and some believe the best chance of eternal life lies with cryonics, a process in which dead bodies are stored at extremely low temperatures in the hope that at some point future technology will be available to revive them and address the causes

SCIENCE AND THE NATURAL WORLD

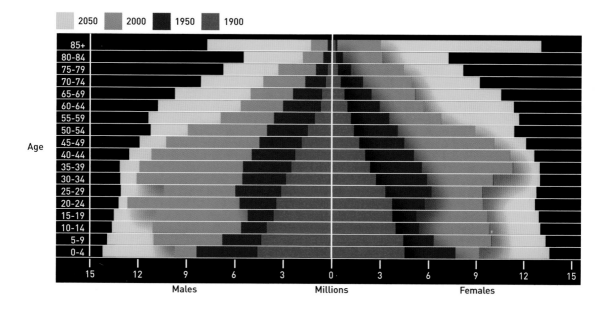

2050   2000   1950   1900

Age

85+
80-84
75-79
70-74
65-69
60-64
55-59
50-54
45-49
40-44
35-39
30-34
25-29
20-24
15-19
10-14
5-9
0-4

15   12   9   6   3   0   3   6   9   12   15

Males   Millions   Females

COLD AS ICE *The cryogenically frozen body of James Bedford (opposite), wrapped in Mylar and placed in a cryo-capsule constructed of steel and aluminium. Bedford, a university professor from California, died in 1967, and his cryogenically preserved remains are the oldest to remain intact to this day. The graph above charts progress in extending life expectancy throughout the 20th century, and extrapolates hopes for the future.*

of their original death. The theory was originally put forward in the early 1960s, and a 73-year-old man became the first person to go into 'cryogenic suspension' in 1967.

It is illegal to put a living person into suspension. However, the legal definition of death as the permanent cessation of the heart allows for the preservation of bodies that still have ongoing cellular brain function. Once death has been confirmed, a cryonics team swings into action. They keep the brain minimally functional as it is transported to a company facility. The body is placed in ice and injected with coagulants to prevent blood clots.

Water is removed from the cells, so that when the body is frozen, welling ice crystals won't split the cell structures as it expands. Instead, it is replaced with a sort of human antifreeze. Packing in ice brings the body temperature down to -130°C (-200°F). The body is then put in an aluminium chamber before going into a larger tank of liquid nitrogen (shared with up to five new friends also in suspension). Here the temperature is maintained at -196°C (-321°F). Then it's just a question of waiting (and of course hoping that someone in the future will eventually be bothered to revive you even if the technology does become available).

Only a handful of companies offer the service, and it is expensive. Aside from a membership fee payable while you're alive, the cost of suspension reportedly ranges from US$50,000 to US$150,000. So far, it's thought that 200 people have gone into suspension, some taking the 'whole body' option and others opting for just their heads. The technology remains in its infancy and thus far no one has been successfully revived. Nonetheless, it offers perhaps the best chance of immortality should it ever emerge from the realms of science fiction.

72

Reproduce the Big Bang

WHAT IT IS The moment at which the cosmos was born
WHY YOU WON'T DO IT Reproducing it too effectively might just bring an end to the Universe

It is a question that has captivated mankind for millennia: how did our world and the Universe around it begin? As far as most of the scientific community is concerned, the answer is that everything began with the Big Bang a little less than 14 billion years ago. Understanding this phenomenon occupies the working lives of thousands of scientists around the world.

The Big Bang theory describes the moment at which our Universe, then an unimaginably hot and dense bubble smaller than an atom, exploded. All that energy rapidly expanded and cooled, creating matter and space and time – in short, all the conditions and materials needed to build our Universe as we know it today. That, then, is the theory but scientists continue to struggle to comprehend just how the process occurred. So might we some day be able to recreate the conditions of the Big Bang and thus answer some of the most fundamental questions of our existence?

The basic building block of our Universe is the atom, consisting of protons, electrons and neutrons. It has only been in relatively recent times (i.e. since the early part of the 20th century) that we have been able to split the atom and increase our understanding of how these subatomic particles work. The problem for those studying the Big Bang is that they are dealing with even smaller building blocks – sub-subatomic particles such as neutrinos and quarks.

However, it is now possible to break down protons and neutrons into quarks and other massless subatomic particles known as gluons. These can exist for just the tiniest fraction of a second before dying in a flash of energy – just long enough for the most cutting-edge gadgetry to observe them.

So how do we go about isolating these subatomic particles that were present in the first few milliseconds of the creation of the universe? For all the technology involved, the basic answer is by using brute force.

The chief bit of equipment needed is a particle accelerator. Often taking up acres of land, these remarkable pieces of kit are the proverbial massive sledgehammers used to crack tiny subatomic nuts. They consist of vast banks of magnets that accelerate proton beams into each other close to the speed of light. In some cases they are simply arranged around a long, straight tunnel (a linear accelerator), while in others they are arranged in a huge doughnut-

SCIENCE AND THE NATURAL WORLD

UP IN THE AIR *Astronauts Peggy Whitson and Valery Korzun juggle hamburgers on the International Space Station during the 'Expedition 5' mission in 2002. The two were part of a crew who undertook some 25 new investigations over their six-month stay aboard the station (shown opposite above the limb of Earth).*

training so that you can work as safely and effectively as possible once in orbit.

If all that sounds too much like hard work, then the alternative is to take the tourist trail. Space tourists pay a premium to spend time on the ISS as civilians (though you'll typically be expected to undertake scientific investigation while you're up there). Those who take this route tend to hate being called space tourists, preferring such terms as 'private space explorer' or 'spaceflight participant' (NASA's euphemism of choice). Tickets don't come cheap. For a stay of up to a couple of weeks, expect to pay in the range of US$25 million to US$40 million. You'll also need to pass a vigorous course of

training, covering much of the same ground as 'proper' astronauts.

American businessman Dennis Tito became the first paying customer to visit the ISS when he joined the crew for eight days in 2001. As of 2013, six others had followed in his footsteps, spending up to 15 days at a time on board. In 2009, IT entrepreneur Charles Simonyi became the first man to go on two missions, racking up a total of 29 days at a combined cost of US$60 million. Every space tourist thus far has been transported to the station on a Russian Soyuz spacecraft. Each trip was arranged by Virginia-based space travel agency Space Adventures.

Just make sure you've got up-to-date insurance – Japanese businessman Daisuke Enomoto paid US$21 million for a 2006 spaceflight, but was ultimately deemed medically unfit to fly. He subsequently sued Space Adventures after he was refused a refund.

Climb Annapurna

There are 14 mountains in the world taller than 8,000 metres (26,240 ft), and Annapurna I, in the Himalayas in Nepal, is only the tenth highest, at 8,091 metres (26,545 ft). Yet it is regarded as the most dangerous climb of all, with some 38 per cent of all climbers who attempt it dying in the process. Fancy your chances?

Annapurna, whose name translates as 'Goddess of the Harvests', was first conquered in 1950, but by 2007 there had only been 153 successful ascents.

Your trip is likely to cost several thousand dollars. Investigate the visa requirements and get a good insurance policy. In addition, make sure you hire one of the best local guides: prone to regular avalanches, this is a climb to be taken on only by experienced mountaineers.

Pokhara is the nearest major city, and the safest time to attempt an ascent is in April or May, but you'll need to start preparing at least a year in advance of that. Work on your cardiovascular fitness by running for an hour a day for four out of every five days. Focus weight-training on your upper body. Keep your climbing skills up to date by, well, climbing, and undertake whatever cold-weather and altitude training you can manage.

You can expect to lose up to 20 per cent of your bodyweight during the climb, so

aim to put on around 6 kilos (1 stone) in weight before you go. In addition, you'll need to prepare yourself psychologically – the climb poses immense challenges and there may be moments when you feel you can't go on, but good mental preparation will help you get through them. You will variously need to cope with stress, boredom, fear, frustration and even hallucinations, all while you are tired and under significant physical strain. As you near the peak, the stress and thin air can reduce your mental alertness by as much as 30 per cent.

Your basic climbing kit should include: a harness, ropes, clips, karabiners and a rappel device; crampons; an ice axe; goggles and headlamp; ski poles; and an altimeter. Other essential equipment includes foot powder; oxygen canisters; satellite phone; two-way radio; a tent; and wet wipes (there'll be no warm baths for a while).

In terms of clothing, you should wear a thermal underlayer, several fleece layers (tops and bottoms), plus a set of

TOP OF THE WORLD

The Annapurna Sanctuary is a high basin some 40 kilometres (25 miles) north of Nepal's second-largest city, Pokhara. Carved out by the powerful forces of glacial erosion, it is hemmed in on all sides by the Annapurna mountain range. Long shadows from these towering peaks mean the basin only gets a few hours of sunshine even in the height of summer.

down trousers and jacket. Wear thick socks, and invest in a pair of frost-proof climbing boots. Kit yourself out in several pairs of gloves, starting with lightweight pairs, then thicker mitts and a final pair of oversized Gore-Tex gloves.

A scarf or bandana will protect your neck from the sun. Wear a hat with ear flaps, and top off with a visor to protect you from the sun and a thin mask worn over the face. You will need two sets of everything: one set to wear during the day and another to wear at night while your climbing garb dries out.

Ensure you keep hydrated and eat enough food. You are likely to burn through 6,000 calories a day. However, the higher you get, the less hungry you will feel. Pack high-energy foods such as chocolate and biscuits, plus boil-in-the-bag foods (which take up less room in your pack). Bring along a sack so you can gather snow to supplement your water supplies. You will also need a small heating appliance and some basic utensils.

Be aware of the risks to your health, so that you can pick up on signs and

respond quickly. Potential ailments include:
• Acute Mountain Sickness (AMS), caused by the body being unable to deal with high altitude and low pressure. This can result in fluid on the brain or in the lungs – look out for flu-like symptoms, insomnia, confusion and 'death rattle' in breathing.
• Alpine trench foot, caused by wet feet.
• Altitude sickness, leaving the sufferer feeling generally poorly as a result of reduced oxygen intake.
• Frostbite, caused by lack of blood flow to extremities. Cloudy white skin tone is an early sign.
• Hypothermia, caused by a fall in the core body temperature, with symptoms ranging from shivering to mental confusion, and death a real threat.

A well-stocked first aid kit is essential. Treat cuts and minor ailments promptly, protect against sunburn, and in the case of broken bones, consider dosing on morphine to reduce pain until you can get help. Take aspirin to thin your blood, which can thicken dangerously with altitude. Finally, remember to treat the Goddess with respect – and enjoy the views.

75 Fight a duel

WHAT IT IS Putting your life on the line as a matter of honour
WHY YOU WON'T DO IT It's illegal, and these days sparring can be done much more safely on social networking sites

For centuries, duelling was the favoured method by which posh people (who should really have known better) settled disputes among themselves. Originally this highly ritualized form of armed combat involved swords, but the pistol later became the weapon of choice. And while you might still be tempted to end your arguments as decisively, there really are better methods.

These days, duelling is illegal virtually everywhere on the planet – even where it's not directly prohibited by legislation, you will likely find yourself charged with murder, attempted murder or

grievous bodily harm. That said, some people never learn. For instance, in 2002 Peruvian congressman Eittel Ramos took umbrage at something said by vice president David Waisman

SHOOT-OUT *A pair of boxed duelling pistols by Trulock & Sons. There was a time during the 18th and 19th centuries when no affluent gentleman would be without a pair of such weapons for those occasions when honour demanded satisfaction.*

and challenged him to a pistol duel. Waisman, not unreasonably, politely turned him down.

In times past, however, this sort of rationality seems to have been in rather short supply. So it was that in 1804 a 'beef' between Aaron Burr, then vice president of the USA, and his political rival Alexander Hamilton culminated in the former shooting the latter dead. Burr avoided facing charges, although the incident also killed his political career. Yet at around this time the duel was still considered so vital to settling disputes and maintaining

social order that it was guarded by a set of strict rules known as the 'Code Duello'.

In order to trigger a duel, one party had to be sufficiently offended to lay down a challenge and 'demand satisfaction'. This was classically done by casting a glove (or gauntlet) onto the floor. At this point, a contest could be avoided if the 'challenged' issued an apology to the challenger for the perceived affront. Even if the challenger had outdone the original slur with a retort of his own, it was the initial slight that required the first apology.

TO THE DEATH *This engraving depicts a duel in the Bois de Boulogne to the west of Paris. Duelling in France was outlawed by Louis XIII as early as 1626, and this convenient park became a popular rendezvous for those who wanted to settle scores without the intervention of the law. The last recorded duel in France was a sword fight between two parliamentarians in 1967.*

The traditional time for a duel was dawn. This timing, along with the selection of a remote 'field of honour', ensured a degree of privacy and, crucially, also gave time for combatants to sleep things off if a challenge was issued when they were a little the worse for wear.

If fighting with swords, the duel could be to the death, until one party was bloodied, disabled or disarmed, or until an apology was offered. If using pistols, the combatants stood back-to-back before walking a set number of paces, turning and firing.

Duelling pistols were, to some extent, designed to miss. They had smooth-barrelled interiors (unlike the grooved barrels of rifles) and used smooth shot, making it hard to be truly accurate. Although the duelling code forbade deliberate misfiring, the duel could be called off if both parties remained unhurt after the first shot. No duel went beyond three rounds – not least because if no one was hit by then, it started to look a bit embarrassing.

In fact, the historical record suggests that the vast majority of duels did not result in fatalities, and a good proportion ended with both parties unscathed but with honour restored. In these more civilized times, of course, we're more likely to settle things over a nice cup of tea and a slice of cake – or failing that, call in the lawyers.

Assuming that an apology was not forthcoming and the challenge was taken up, the challenged person now had the right to select weapons. Anybody with a bit of common sense would have gone for something like pea-shooters or a round or two of 'scissors, paper, stone', but, somewhat mystifyingly, the sword and the pistol were always more popular.

Each duellist appointed a 'second', a trusted friend who made sure things were organized properly and weapons prepared and ready. The seconds might also have striven to smooth over the dispute even at this late stage.

76 Learn Linear A

WHAT IT IS An undeciphered language of the ancients
WHY YOU WON'T DO IT Unfortunately, there's no 'Rosetta Stone' to give you a kick-start

If you're the kind of person who thinks you have a gift for languages because you can read a menu in French and book a hotel in Spanish, then perhaps you'd like to flex those linguistic muscles in a new direction? How about trying to make sense of Linear A – a rediscovered ancient language that has stumped armies of academics for more than a century.

Linear A was a language used on the Mediterranean island of Crete between the 18th and 15th centuries BC, during the heyday of the spectacular ancient Minoan civilization. It seems to have been the forerunner of another language with links to ancient Greek – the imaginatively named Linear B – and may have been used primarily for government and religious records.

Both languages were rediscovered by the famed British archaeologist Arthur Evans in the early 1900s, on artefacts uncovered during his excavations at the Cretan palace of Knossos. Both scripts incorporate 'ideographic' signs (symbols representing entire objects or ideas, similar to Egyptian hieroglyphs) but are also the first known European languages using symbols to denote syllables.

Linear B inscriptions on material such as ceramics and stone tablets were significantly more plentiful than Linear A writings, giving academics an obvious advantage in translating the former language, but it still took until the 1950s for a young English architect and language prodigy called Michael Ventris to decipher Linear B. The key to his discovery was the realization that it shared some common ground with ancient Greek (a trait not shared by Linear A). Lacking a convenient 'Rosetta Stone'-style inscription to show him the same text in multiple languages, Ventris managed to unlock Linear B without having any idea what any of the scripts said – a unique achievement.

Alas, Ventris died tragically young in a car accident just three years after conquering Linear B and before he could master Linear A. And although the two languages share some symbols, no one has yet worked out for sure which other languages Linear A may be related to. Some suggest a link to the ancient Luwian language, others to archaic Phoenician languages or perhaps to the language of the Etruscans. However, these links represent nothing more than avenues for investigation and the goal of unlocking Linear A seems as far off as ever.

77 Eat fire

WHAT IT IS One hot meal you don't want to consume
WHY YOU WON'T DO IT Get it wrong, and it'll do more than just make your eyes water

We all know just how painful it can be when you burn your tongue on a hot drink, so why would you ever want to stick a flaming torch in your mouth? Despite appearances, however, the celebrated circus skill of fire-eating need not cause you any damage – provided you know *exactly* what you're doing!

First, a word of warning – fire-eating is the kind of thing that looks cool (if you'll pardon the pun), and might seem like a good idea when you're under the influence. Under no circumstances attempt the feat in this condition. Instead, treat it as a serious skill and get proper training from an expert – many circus schools offer courses. The trick is to extinguish the torch by using your mouth to cut off the fire's oxygen supply. Practise the techniques with an unlit skewer at first – it's all about controlling your breathing. When the torch goes in your mouth, on no account breath in – doing so will inhale fire and fuel vapours into your lungs, causing permanent damage or even death. Practise your breathing techniques, and never perform if you are puffed out.

Choose your equipment carefully: kerosene is a good fuel option, while petrol, with its tendency to explode, is not. Kevlar wicks are better than cotton. Avoid wearing baggy clothes, tie back your hair and make sure onlookers are at a safe distance. Keep a wet rag, a fire extinguisher and a first aid kit to hand. The ideal location is a high-ceilinged, well-ventilated room with a non-flammable floor. If outside, beware of unpredictable wind conditions. Remember that heat rises – keep the flame above you throughout your act.

Once the torch is alight, check for rogue gusts of wind or draughts. If conditions are satisfactory, lift the torch above your head. Stand with your legs apart so you are balanced, shrug your shoulders and tilt your head back until your mouth and throat face straight up. Wet your lips and take a breath in. That way, if you are given a shock you can only exhale. Now stick out your tongue wide and flat, lowering the torch onto it. Take the flames into your mouth, being careful not to inhale. Close your lips around the torch to cut off the oxygen supply, but not so tightly that you make contact with the hot metal shaft of the torch. With a final puff out, extinguish the flames. Be prepared for some burns to the mouth and lips as you perfect your skills. For anything serious, seek medical attention.

Play Rachmaninoff's Third

You might feel that once you've mastered 'Chopsticks', the piano has no further musical challenges left to offer you. But many classically trained pianists agree that the pinnacle of difficulty actually lies in mastering the fiendish Third Piano Concerto of Russian composer Sergei Rachmaninoff.

Composed in 1909, Rachmaninoff's Piano Concerto No. 3 in D Minor (Op. 30, for those who care about such things) has three movements. He dedicated the work to the Polish-American pianist, Josef Hofmann, but Hofmann never actually played it in public as he considered it wasn't for him. So who actually is it for?

As you might have guessed, this is not a piece for beginners. You will need many years of experience behind you before it is even worth attempting. But conversely, some of the greatest pianists have believed it's best to take it on while you still have youth on your side. As Gary Graffman (the American musician perhaps best known for his rendering of Gershwin's 'Rhapsody in Blue' for Woody Allen's *Manhattan*) said, he wished he'd learned the piece when he was 'still too young to know fear'. If you want to understand what he meant, watch *Shine*, the 1996 Oscar-winning movie starring Geoffrey Rush as schizophrenic musical prodigy David Helfgott, whose attempts to master the piece led to a breakdown.

You will need big hands. Rachmaninoff had them and, as the old saying goes, big hands are an indicator of... an ability to span a lot of piano keys. In simple terms, Rachmaninoff crammed a lot of notes into every bar, so you will need to build up the muscle memory in your fingers to hit them all. Stamina is also essential: the piece lasts a good half-hour, and the pianist barely takes a pause for the duration. In addition, the music is unpredictable from moment to moment and you will need to employ your full concentration. And alongside technical ability, you'll also need passion and personality. This is an emotionally draining piece.

Don't worry if you don't get it all right. Consider the wise words of the comic genius Eric Morecambe responding to criticism from composer André Previn: 'I'm playing all the right notes... but not necessarily in the right order.' And if you do manage to get to grips with Concerto No. 3, why not move on to No. 2, which even Rachmaninoff himself famously found 'uncomfortable to play'?

79 Karate chop a wooden block

WHAT IT IS Shattering timber with soft flesh
WHY YOU WON'T DO IT Get it wrong and it's your hand that breaks – not the wood

If you've ever seen a martial arts movie, then surely you occasionally dream of unleashing a lightning-fast karate chop and amazing everyone with your hidden prowess? With the right training, you too could imitate the moves of Bruce Lee and Jackie Chan – but please try to keep it for inanimate objects rather than trying it on any humans.

Karate is just one of many Japanese martial arts, developed from the native skills practised in the Riyuku islands of what is now Okinawa Prefecture. Like most martial arts, it is in fact a complex blend of philosophy and fighting. However, the violent martial arts movies of the 1970s that saw it shoot to worldwide fame owed their popularity mostly to the impressive physical feats achieved by the protagonists.

If you want to amaze your friends and perhaps find inner calm, then you'll need to train with a martial arts expert who can help you develop the necessary skills. You will likely use a canvas punch bag to help toughen your hands and so avoid cuts. Your master will advise you on what you can attempt at any stage. With instruction, a near-beginner can usually generate a chop speed of 6 metres (20 ft) per second – enough to break a 2.5-centimetre (1-in) wooden board. A black belt, meanwhile, might manage 14 metres (46 ft) per second, generating enough force to smash through 4 centimetres (1.5 in) of concrete.

Karate's signature move, the chop (also known as the knifehand strike or, in Japanese, *shutō-uchi*) involves using the underside of your hand to shatter through a plank of wood. Your little finger should be parallel to the ground and your thumb should be bent so that its end rests at the base of your index finger. As you strike, your fingers should be slightly bent (towards the left if you are using your right hand, or to the right if you are using your left).

When setting up your chop, balance the wood between stable supports. Stand a couple of feet back, with your feet about a shoulders' width apart. Alternatively, kneel so that your knees line up with your shoulders. As you prepare to strike, relax yourself and focus on the task in hand. Abort the attempt if you are distracted. Visualize successfully breaking through the wood. You should aim for an imaginary point a little below the plank itself, so that you strike it before the chop starts to slow. Raise your arm high in the air then bring down the hand in a rapid, smooth stroke.

196   TESTS OF SKILL AND DARING

80 Catch a bullet

WHAT IT IS One of the most impressive feats in the magician's canon
WHY YOU WON'T DO IT All the preparation in the world cannot ensure your safety

It is one of the most spectacular and dangerous tricks in the illusionist's armoury, in which the intrepid performer apparently uses his hand or mouth to pluck from mid-air a bullet fired from a gun. Done properly, there should be no risk to anyone involved – but be warned, accidents do happen...

The first accounts of this very old trick date back to the early 17th century. Over the centuries, it is said to have accounted for more than a dozen magicians taking their final curtain call – including the celebrated Original Chinese Conjurer Chung Ling Soo (real name William Ellsworth Robinson), killed in 1918 when a gun misfired during a show at London's Wood Green Empire. So this is really not a suitable situation for just 'giving it a go' and hoping that everything works out. Train with an expert, learn his or her secrets, and don't attempt the trick itself until you know success is guaranteed. Even then, wear bullet-proof clothing in case of accidents.

The trick should run as follows:
• The magician asks a member of the audience to inspect the firearm and nstructs them to mark a bullet with their initials.
• An assistant then loads the bullet into the gun in front of the audience.
• The magician stands on one side of the stage, the assistant on the other. The assistant aims and fires the gun.

• Many performers place a sheet of glass between themselves and the gun so that the audience can see the glass smash as the bullet passes through it.
• The magician collapses to the floor as if the bullet has struck them. (Hopefully, he or she will be acting by this point...)
• Finally, they stagger to their feet and reveal the bullet safely ensconced in one hand or clenched between the teeth, much to the audience's relief.

So how is it done? The secret is to use a wax bullet. Once the original (non-wax) bullet has been marked by an audience member, switch it over by sleight of hand. Secrete it in your hand or mouth while the assistant loads the wax bullet. When this is fired, it should be robust enough to break the glass, but won't do you any permanent damage even if it does strike you.

Just make sure your team knows exactly which are the real bullets and which are the duds – and be careful not to upset your assistant, since you're literally putting your life in his or her hands!

81 Spacewalk

WHAT IT IS An amble through the cosmos
WHY YOU WON'T DO IT You might prefer somewhere with a little more atmosphere

There can be few more potent symbols of mankind's great scientific achievements than the sight of a human being floating in space. Those in the business don't actually call it spacewalking, however, but rather EVA (extravehicular activity). And it's not all about adventure – even in space you need to wee.

The first man to go on an EVA was Soviet cosmonaut, Aleksei Leonov, who made a 12-minute walk on 18 March 1965 and ran into difficulties when his spacesuit expanded and he had to struggle to fit back through the airlock. Another Russian, Anatoly Solovyev, has more experience of floating in the great beyond than anybody else, with 82 hours and 16 EVAs under his belt.

Training takes place in vast water tanks that simulate the weightless conditions of orbit. NASA's Neutral Buoyancy Laboratory in Houston, Texas contains some 28 million litres (6.2 million gallons) of water, and astronauts train here for an average of seven hours for every hour they expect to spacewalk. Modern astronauts also take advantage of virtual reality to replicate various spacewalk activities.

Obviously you'll need a spacesuit – or as NASA insists, 'extravehicular mobility unit' (EMU). The suit is designed to protect you from the effects of vacuum, as well as other hazards such as small meteors, extreme temperatures and ultraviolet radiation. EMUs comprise 18 separate parts and 14 distinct layers, and include an in-suit drink bag. The first piece to go on is the MAG (Maximum Absorption Garment), designed to help out if you get caught short in mid-EVA. It takes around 15 minutes to put on the complete suit, but you will spend a full day preparing for a walk. This includes several hours breathing pure oxygen (ridding the body of excess nitrogen and reducing the risk of 'the bends' and a period of decompression in the airlock.

In space, a safety tether around your waist will keep you connected to your vessel at all times. The tether allows you to wander up to 17 metres (55 ft) away. You will also sport a joystick-controlled, jetpack-like device known as SAFER (Simplified Aid for EVA Rescue) to help you get back to your craft if the tether breaks. Depending on the complexity of your task, the walk may last anything from a few minutes to several hours, but however hard you're working, remember to stop and enjoy the view.

82 Saw someone in half

WHAT IT IS A classic stage magic stunt
WHY YOU WON'T DO IT The consequences of a slip of the hand are unthinkable

Legend has it that this popular illusion was first performed by a magician named Torrini in 1809 for the delight of Pope Pius VII. Fortunately, no humans need be injured in the making of this dazzling spectacle. A foot model who is willing to maintain their anonymity, however, may come in handy...

Nice though the story is, there is sadly no contemporary evidence for the tale of Torrini performing his trick for dubious papal pleasure. The first properly documented performance took place at St George's Hall in London as recently as 1920, when one P.T. Selbit entertained an invited audience by locking his assistant in a large wooden case. The coffin-like cabinet was then lifted onto a set of trestles, with Selbit seemingly sawing through the assistant's midriff, before pulling the sections of the box apart. The assistant was then released from the box and, to everyone's delight, was shown to be unharmed.

The next great development came in 1921, when an American magician called Horace Goldin worked out how to keep the assistant's head and feet visible for the duration. Blessed with a well-developed business brain, Goldin secured a patent for his technology and effectively blocked other illusionists from practising the trick in the USA for several years. But unfortunately for him, by applying for the patent he necessarily put his technology into the public domain, allowing anyone interested enough to read all about it. In subsequent decades, the trick has been performed in ever slicker and more impressive forms, but you can still turn heads (and perhaps a few stomachs) with the Goldin method described below.

Most importantly, you need a pair of assistants. Tradition says that they should be pretty, female and quite scantily clad (though in this age of equal opportunities, there's no reason not to bisect men if you so choose). You'll also need a specially designed wooden cabinet, and a deeper-than-normal table with a hollowed-out top. At the midpoint of the box, there needs to be a footrest that stops about halfway down the cabinet's depth. The bottom half of the cabinet has a discreet trap door that exactly aligns with a similar trap door in the top of the table, plus two holes from which the feet appear. The top half of the cabinet has a hole big enough so that a head may stick out of it.

202   TESTS OF SKILL AND DARING

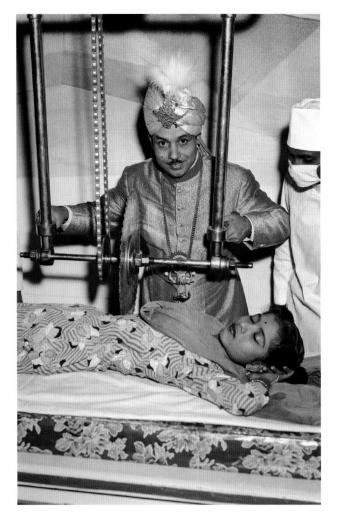

THIS MAY HURT A LITTLE *P.C. Sorcar was an Indian magician who achieved international fame before his death in 1971. Here he is seen during a performance in Paris – fortunately the onlooker in the surgical mask is just there to add an extra frisson of danger!*

Now comes the 'magic'. As Assistant One takes up position, spin the table so that the audience can see her head at one end and feet at the other. While the feet end is out of sight for the audience, Assistant One contorts herself so that her own feet are nestling on the footrest, while Assistant Two pokes her feet through the trap doors and pops them out through the holes at the bottom of the cabinet (giving the toes a flamboyant wiggle for good measure as they come back into the audience's view).

Using whatever sawing device you prefer, cut through the middle of the cabinet, just along from the underside of the footrest. You're effectively cutting through thin air inside the cabinet but Assistant One might like to crank up the tension by giving a blood-curdling scream or two. Now insert a couple of metal plates to hide the cabinet's interior from view – your audience should believe this is to protect them from the terrible, bloody mess held therein. Finally, pull the top half of the cabinet away from the bottom, and enjoy the gasps of the enraptured crowd.

After milking the applause for as long as you feel comfortable, put the two halves of the cabinet back together again. Remove the metal plates and give the cabinet a tap so that Assistant Two knows she should hide her feet back in the table top. Assistant One can now emerge completely unscathed from the cabinet to yet more applause and general adulation.

Before your audience arrives, one of your assistants (let's assume you're a traditionalist, and call her Assistant Two) needs to secrete herself in the hollowed out table top.

With the audience in place and yearning to be amazed, introduce Assistant One. Over-the-top hand gestures and other signs of flamboyance are not essential but they always go down well and can help distract the audience from thinking too much about what else is going on. Now open the sturdy locks on the lid of the cabinet and swing it open, allowing Assistant One to slip gracefully into the cabinet.

83 Go over Niagara Falls in a barrel

WHAT IT IS An act of derring-do at the world's most famous waterfalls
WHY YOU WON'T DO IT There's a big risk that they'll be scraping the bottom of the barrel once they find your remains

One of the world's great sites of natural beauty, you can view Niagara Falls from any number of comfortable spots. Alternatively, you can take the famous *Maid of the Mist* cruise at the foot of the falls, or even fly over them in a helicopter. Not floating your boat? Well, if you want a really intimate view there is another alternative...

Niagara Falls sit on the border between Canada and New York State, and actually consists of three separate falls: the Horseshoe Falls on the Canadian side and the smaller American Falls and Bridal Veil Falls on the New York side. The most impressive are the Horseshoe Falls, some 790 metres (2,600 ft) wide, and with a drop of 53 metres (173 ft) into the wild and freezing waters. Some 2.27 million litres (600,000 gallons) pour through each second, having come via four of the five Great Lakes.

The first person to come up with the idea of going over the Falls in a barrel was a retired schoolteacher by the name of Annie Edson Taylor, who decided to celebrate her 63rd birthday in this unusual style. Rather unfairly, she decided to test her specially adapted pickle barrel before use with her cat Iagara. The unwilling feline guinea-pig survived with only a small cut to the head, and the redoubtable Ms Taylor followed two days later on 24 October 1901. She survived 40 minutes in the barrel, emerging with a cut forehead to

match that of her cat, and lived on for another two decades, eventually being laid to rest in the 'stunters' section' of nearby Oakwood Cemetery. So how might you follow in her wake?

Firstly, consider your motivation. Do you have a death wish? If so, get professional help or lie down in a darkened room until the feeling passes. Aside from deliberate suicides, 15 others have purposely hurled themselves over the Falls since Annie Taylor, in a variety of more or less robust vessels. Many of them were apparently motivated by the promise of fame and fortune, and five of them have died in the process, but how many of them can you name?

These days, it's a criminal offence to go 'stunting without a licence' at the Falls, carrying a fine of up to CA$10,000. The authorities have shown little sympathy to impromptu daredevils over the years – for instance, in 2003 a gent by the name of Kirk Jones went over without a barrel and survived, even turning down a lift back to shore

TESTS OF SKILL AND DARING

FALLING HERO *At left, a view of the imposing falls. Opposite: William 'Red' Hill, the self-proclaimed 'Master Hero of Niagara', prepares to navigate the falls for a third time in 1931. Hill rose to fame after saving the life of another Niagara stunter, Bobby Leach, in 1910, and is credited with saving some 28 people from drowning in and around the falls.*

of drowning in ice-cold water – Annie Taylor was only retrieved some 20 minutes after her plunge, and reportedly found the wait for rescue the most terrifying part of her ordeal. Some of the barrel-rollers have fitted straps inside their barrels to give them increased stability, and many have also added ballast (often, bizarrely, in the form of anvils) to ensure they go over feet first. These precautions backfired fatally for Englishman Charles Stephens, who in 1920 became the first person to die in an attempt. On hitting the water, the anvil that he had tied to his feet went through the base of the barrel, taking the ill-fated Stephens with it. When the barrel was retrieved, a rather gruesome discovery was made – Stephens's right arm was still strapped to the interior.

There are several theories as to why certain attempts succeed. Some say it's about going into the water quite close to the lip of the Falls, so you don't build up excessive speed on the run in. Others posit that there are 'water cones' offering soft landing zones at the base of the Falls, though whether you encounter these seems more a matter of luck than judgement. Another theory suggests that those who succeed effectively 'ride' the water, much like a surfer rides a wave. Except, of course, they're doing it on vertical water, as it were. Quite how you can knowingly 'ride' while crammed into a barrel is a further question that has not yet been adequately explored.

from the *Maid of the Mist*. He was fined CA$2,300 for his efforts, and banned from ever entering Canada again, whether via waterfall or other means.

So what of the physical risks? The barrels used have all been robust and specially strengthened for the job, but regardless of how much padding is put inside, you'll still get buffeted about, leading to risks of broken bones, cuts, bruises and concussion, not to mention being dashed on rocks. This is one reason why all the successful descents have gone over the Horseshoe Falls – they are relatively boulder-free compared to the rockier American Falls.

If you come through the actual descent, you still have to contend with the threat

84 Crack a safe

WHAT IT IS The pinnacle of the bank robber's craft
WHY YOU WON'T DO IT You should rarely have legitimate reason to practise

Safecracking is one of those things that looks easy when you see a dashing cat burglar deftly twisting a dial back and forth in the movies until they hear that telltale 'click' – but what if it's you that needs to steal evidence from some supervillain's headquarters (or, heaven forbid, liberate a diamond necklace)?

The principal tool in a safe-breaker's armoury is time. Whichever approach you decide upon, none of them are speedy. Your first method is to guess the combination: some safes may have well over a million potential combinations, but according to the professionals, people are often remarkably predictable, basing their apparently random codes on birthdays, phone numbers and other easily discovered sequences. Others forget to change the standard combinations set by the manufacturer, and some keep a note of the combination near the safe in case they forget it.

Assuming you don't get lucky in this way, then drilling through the safe can expose the lock so you can manipulate it with a punch rod. However, many manufacturers employ cobalt plates to counter all but the toughest drill bits, while others effectively booby-trap the lock so that a further set of locks is activated to secure the safe.

Few safes are a match for a controlled explosion. The only problem with this approach is that the contents are likely to suffer just as much as the safe. There are similar problems inherent in using, for instance, an oxyacetylene torch, plasma cutters or a thermic lance.

Safe-breakers in the movies use sound, feel and patience. You need to be attuned to tiny clicks that give clues to the combination. This is a real art, and since it's also Hollywood's method of choice, it's worth exploring in more detail.

Rotary locks found in safes consist of a series of anywhere from two to eight wheels (one wheel for each digit in the combination). The combination dial on the front of the safe is connected to the wheels inside by a spindle, which is also connected to a drive cam. Each wheel has a single notch on its edge. The aim is to position all of the wheels so that the notches line up at the top. This will create a gap into which will fall a small metal bar called the fence. It is the fence that, when the notches are unaligned, sits in the way of the bolt, and prevents the door from being opened.

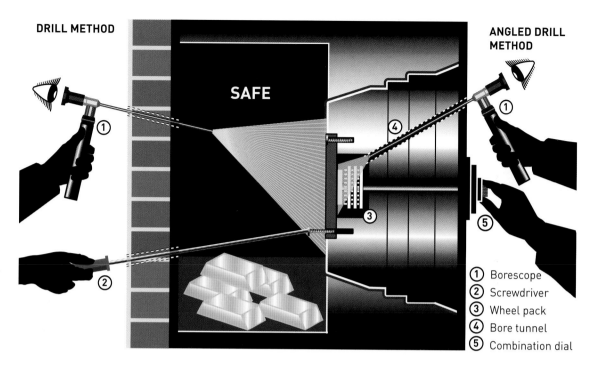

DRILL METHOD

SAFE

ANGLED DRILL METHOD

① Borescope
② Screwdriver
③ Wheel pack
④ Bore tunnel
⑤ Combination dial

DRILLING TECHNIQUES *Specialist drills can offer a shortcut into some safes. After drilling from the front at an angle that avoids protective plates (angled drill method, right), the safecracker can use a borescope to see the wheels in motion as they turn the dial. Alternatively (drill method, left), drilling into the back of safe can provide access to the back of the lock to directly manipulate the wheels..*

In 1940, Harry C. Miller came up with a method that remains the basis of lock manipulation to this day. Firstly, the safe cracker needs to work out where the contact points are on each wheel. These are the points where the lever attached to the fence brushes against the notch, and can be identified by a quiet click.

Having found the contact points on the drive cam, the burglar notes the corresponding numbers on the dial. He or she sets the dial to the number opposite the midpoint of the contact point numbers, then slowly turns the wheel to the right and listens for a series of clicks after going through the contact point numbers. The number of clicks tells him how many wheels there are (and how long the combination is).

Next, the dial is set to zero and turned to the left. The breaker listens once more for the telltale clicks of the contact areas and notes the numbers. This process is repeated, moving the starting point a few numbers to the left each time. The contact area numbers will be slightly different each time. Eventually, the breaker has all the figures he or she needs, and will plot them on a graph, one for the left contact points and one for the right. There should be as many points of convergence as there are wheels. Noting the points of convergence, the breaker now has a finite number of numbers to try out. For example, three numbers have six potential combinations, while six numbers have 720 combinations. That's still quite a lot, but considerably fewer than if you had no reference points.

Yes, it's a lot more complicated than it looks when George Clooney's doing it, but then again, getting into a safe is not supposed to be a walk in the park!

Space dive

WHAT IT IS Free falling
from outside the Earth's
atmosphere
WHY YOU WON'T DO IT
The threat of
decompression sickness,
unconsciousness,
haemorrhaging, hard
ground – you decide!

These days, skydiving is a hugely popular sport – despite the fact that it involves flinging yourself out of a plane, plummeting for a bit and then entrusting your fate to a flimsy combination of cord and canvas. Space divers take it to the next level, hitching a ride to jaw-dropping altitudes, and re-entering Earth's atmosphere on their way back to the ground.

So far, space diving has been something of a niche sport. Its earliest exponent was US Air Force captain Joseph Kittinger, who in 1959 and 1960 made a series of record-breaking leaps from a capsule suspended below a helium balloon as part of Project Excelsior. This USAF programme (whose name, fittingly, meant 'ever higher') aimed to test a multi-stage parachute system designed to save pilots in high-altitude bailouts. Kittinger's space-diving career culminated on 16 August 1960, when he leapt from some 31,300 metres (102,800 ft), free-falling for 4 minutes and 36 seconds before triggering his main parachutes.

Kittinger's record stood for more than five decades, but was broken in 2012 by Austrian daredevil Felix Baumgartner. In contrast to Kittinger's jumps, which were only publicized after their successful completion, Baumgartner made his leap amid the unrelenting attention of a global publicity blitz, with only a 20-second time delay on the 'live' camera feeds in case disaster struck.

What's more, although Baumgartner's leap was designed to collect scientific data to help in the design of future high-altitude pressure suits, it was sponsored not by an aerospace agency, but by a soft drinks firm. The Red Bull Stratos project, to give it its full name, was years in the planning, and required deep pockets and the involvement of a huge team of professionals, from scientists and engineers to coaches and, of course, media managers.

Baumgartner, who had already made a name for himself through other feats of aerial daring (see page 51) broke the long-standing record in style with a leap from 39,000 metres (128,000 ft or more than 23 miles). Installed within a 1.8-metre (6-ft) diameter capsule suspended beneath a balloon, it took him just under three hours to climb to this altitude on 14 October 2012. Here, he leapt from the very edge of outer space, falling back through the vast majority of Earth's atmosphere. During his descent, Baumgartner reached speeds of 1,358 kilometres per hour

SPACE FALL *Austrian daredevil Felix Baumgartner jumps from his specially designed capsule and into legend. He made his headline-grabbing leap from 39 kilometres (23 miles) above Roswell, New Mexico, on 14 October 2012.*

(844 mph or Mach 1.24), becoming the first human to break the sound barrier without mechanical aid. After a little more than 9 minutes of descent (including 4 minutes and 19 seconds in free fall), he touched down safely in the New Mexico desert.

So if you harbour ambitions to break Baumgartner's record, and can find someone to back your ambition with a big investment, what lessons should you take on board from his experience? First off, you'll need a huge amount of skydiving experience before you even think of it – falling very fast might not seem that difficult, but you need to manage your descent, steering yourself onto a stable trajectory and above all

avoiding the kind of rapid spins that could cause you to black out and even suffer haemorrhaging.

Patience is a virtue: helium balloons are delicate beasts and you'll need perfect conditions for your ascent, so expect lots of delays and postponements. Train yourself to relax, and especially to cope with claustrophobia – during ascent you will be stuck in a tiny capsule, in a highly restrictive pressure suit, for several hours. Make sure you have a friendly and trustworthy voice to talk to on the ground – Baumgartner's team recruited Joseph Kittinger himself to act as his coach and the calm voice of 'ground control'.

Don't expect to come back as quite the same person you were when you left. For Baumgartner, the experience was profound: 'Sometimes you have to go up really high to understand how small you really are.'

86 Free solo up the Eiffel Tower

WHAT IT IS Climbing unaided up the Paris landmark
WHY YOU WON'T DO IT Most of us don't have that kind of head for heights

In the world of climbing, 'free soloing' is about as difficult and dangerous as it gets. Regular climbers may call upon all manner of ropes and specialist equipment to aid their ascents. Free climbers, meanwhile, only use kit to safeguard against falls. Soloing, though, allows for no equipment at all.

The discipline when practised on man-made structures is also known as 'buildering'. Quite when the daredevil art began is unknown, though there is a strong case to identify the British climber and author Geoffrey Winthrop Young as its spiritual founder – he left detailed records of his jaunts up the various buildings of Cambridge University in the late 19th century.

Common sense will tell you that free soloing is not something to be approached lightly. In fact, it should not be practised by anybody who is not a highly experienced and skilled traditional climber: this is not a sport for beginners. Great climbers are likely to have a strong back, a vice-like grip and great coordination. They will also be masters of advanced climbing techniques – skills that have become instinctive through thousands of hours of practice.

For those who feel ready to take on the challenge, free soloing is as much about maintaining concentration and achieving the necessary frame of mind as it is about physical prowess. The lack of safety equipment means that there is no room for error. The chances are that if you fall, you will fall only once – and over the years, the sport has claimed the lives of several of its most famous practitioners. Pushing at your own limits is all well and good, but only the most reckless climber would take on a challenge without knowing if it is within his or her capabilities. Responsible soloists climb routes that they already know they have the skills to complete. That is to say, they climb within their limits. Indeed, they may well have previously climbed a proposed route with safety equipment in order to map out and understand the particular challenges it presents.

So why target the Eiffel Tower in particular? It is by no means the tallest structure in the world, nor necessarily the most challenging to scale. It is, however, an icon, and as such has tempted several climbers over the years. Designed by Gustave Eiffel for the World's Fair held in Paris in 1889, the

TESTS OF SKILL AND DARING   **213**

TESTS OF SKILL AND DARING

OFF THE SCALE *Alain Robert scaled the Eiffel Tower (opposite) on New Year's Eve in 1996, later describing its famous iron framework as 'nothing but a big ladder'. Here (left), he is seen in 2007 preparing for the more challenging ascent of Dubai's Burj Khalifa – some three times the height of the famous Parisian landmark.*

is Alain Robert, also known as the French Spiderman. He made his Eiffel ascent in the late 1990s, adding it to a list of conquests that includes the Empire State Building, the Golden Gate Bridge, the Petronas Towers in Kuala Lumpur and the world's tallest building, the Burj Khalifa in Dubai (see page 12).

Most of Robert's ascents have been illegal, and he typically catches security off their guard by beginning at around dawn, but he has also been paid to scale various buildings for publicity purposes (for instance, the six-hour Burj Khalifa climb was officially sanctioned – and Robert did agree to use a harness to meet safety requirements). Rumour has it that the owners of The Shard in London, currently the tallest building in western Europe, have put an injunction in place to prevent the Spiderman from getting too close.

For anyone brave, or perhaps foolhardy, enough to join the select group of Eiffel Tower climbers, there are a few basic tips to take on board:
• Invest in the best-quality climbing shoes you can afford.
• Carry a bag of climbing chalk on your person to keep your hands dry and improve your grip.
• Await good weather conditions – the climb will be hard enough at the best of times. Rain or, heaven forbid, ice, will make it all but impossible.
• Finally, take your time. Rush and you'll probably be hurrying to your end.

Tower is the most visited paying visitor attraction in the world. An external climb is certainly one way of avoiding the lengthy queues that can often be seen snaking from the ticket booths.

However, free solo climbing up the 273 metres (896 ft) to the top floor without authorization is against the law. Anyone who does it can expect to be rewarded with a prompt arrest and quite probably a fine or even a jail sentence. In November 2007, English climber Mike Robertson was arrested a little over 200 metres (656 ft) into an ascent of the Tower, which he said he was making to bring attention to the plight of the Burmese people. Starting at the Tower's southeast foot, he had spent some 50 minutes climbing, and a further 20 minutes hiding from the authorities.

Perhaps the most famous climber to have ascended the Tower, however,

Steal the Crown Jewels

WHAT IT IS Perhaps the ultimate crime caper
WHY YOU WON'T DO IT There is no better guarded treasure on the planet

As you might expect, it has never been very easy to get your hands on the Crown Jewels of the British monarchy, although there have been a few notable attempts over the years. If you're thinking of giving it a go today, you will find security better than ever – but there are still lessons to be learned from the attempts of the past.

The Crown Jewels of the United Kingdom are estimated to be worth something in the region of £13 billion (US$20 billion). The centrepiece Imperial State Crown (made in 1838 for Queen Victoria and shown opposite) includes the Black Prince's Ruby, a jewel the size of a hen's egg given to the famous son of Edward III in 1367, alongside some 2,818 diamonds, 297 pearls and assorted other gems. It weighs in at a neck-straining 0.9 kilograms (2 lb). The Sceptre with the Cross, meanwhile, houses the Cullinan I diamond (or 'Great Star of Africa'), a 530-carat beauty cut from the largest diamond ever mined. Or perhaps you prefer the rather less showy 186-carat Koh-i-Noor, the second largest cut diamond in the world, which now sits in the1937 Crown of Queen Elizabeth?

The Crown Jewels have resided at the Tower of London since 1303 – brought to this most secure of royal castles after an attempted theft from their previous home at Westminster Abbey. Since 1994 they have been housed in a specially constructed Jewel House at Waterloo Barracks, where they can be viewed by 2,500 people per hour. They lie on French velvet, behind 5-centimetre-thick (2-in) reinforced glass, and even if you breached the casing, your chances of eluding the entire Tower Guard and the Yeomen Warders are remote. But things weren't always this secure, and the most famous attempted theft of all, carried out by the enticingly named Colonel Blood, came perilously close to success.

Anglo-Irish soldier Thomas Blood conceived his audacious scheme in 1671, at a time when the jewels were open for inspection in the Martin Tower at the Tower of London by paying the custodian. In late spring, Blood visited the Tower disguised as a parson and in the company of a female accomplice who pretended to be his wife. While viewing the jewels, the 'wife' feigned stomach cramps, at which point the elderly Master of the Jewel House, one Talbot Edwards, hurried off to get her a tonic. Mrs Edwards took pity on Mrs Blood and invited her to recover in their apartment. Over the following weeks, an

IMPENETRABLE FORTRESS *A view across the substantial walls of the Tower of London towards the central White Tower, built on the orders of William the Conqueror in the late 11th century. Today the British Crown Jewels are kept in the Jewel House at Waterloo Barracks, just opposite the White Tower and under constant guard.*

apparent friendship blossomed between the two couples. Eventually, as was the way of things back then, Blood even suggested that his nephew might be a fitting husband for the Edwards's daughter

On 9 May, Blood arranged for another viewing of the Crown Jewels, this time in the company of his 'nephew' and two other companions. They carried canes containing blades and assorted other weapons. While one of the thieves stood guard, the others attacked Edwards, throwing a cloak over him and beating and stabbing him, before tying him up

and gagging him. The metal grille that protected the jewels was then removed and the men made a grab for whatever they could carry, mutilating the regalia where necessary in order to conceal it upon their persons.

As luck would have it, Edwards's son stumbled upon the raid just as his father managed to free himself from his bindings. They raised the alarm, and Blood and his men fled with several warders in pursuit. Blood was soon caught and the stolen finery retrieved. Bound in chains, he was hauled before the king but, to general bemusement, secured himself not only a royal pardon but a tidy estate in Ireland to boot. It has been suggested that the king was won over by Blood's shameless bravado, but anyone attempting a similar ruse today can expect rather less lenient treatment.

88 Make a ramp-to-ramp motorcycle jump

WHAT IT IS The most impressive thing you can do on two wheels
WHY YOU WON'T DO IT Evel Knievel broke 433 bones in his body – and he was the best there ever was...

In the 1970s, stunt motorcyclist Evel Knievel was an American icon and one of the most famous people in the world, adored for his daredevil feats but known as much for his dramatic failures as his spectacular successes. If you want to follow in his trail of burnt rubber, you'll need to summon up your deepest reserves of bravery, athleticism and focus.

Before starting down this road, it's worth noting that alongside his numerous distance-jumping records, Knievel still retains one rather unenviable entry in the *Guiness World Records* – that for recovering from most broken bones (433 to be precise). The sobering lesson is that, whatever you stand to gain from a career as a stunt jumper, and however brilliant you become, you can expect a lot of pain, too.

Firstly, you need to be sure you want to be a jumper. It's no good falling in love with the idea but then discovering, as a ramp looms up in front of you, that you'd rather be at home playing tiddlywinks. You must be in physically good shape and mentally strong, and obviously have a pretty fearless disposition. The ability to ride a motorbike helps, of course, but successful jumps largely rely on going hell for leather in a straight line, so don't worry if you're not so good at cornering.

Invest in the right gear – it might very well save your life. Go for top-quality leathers, and make sure they have a built-in spine protector. Get the best helmet you can afford, tough gloves and boots, and pads for your elbows, knees and shins. All your clothing will need to be fire-resistant too.

Choice of bike is a matter of personal taste, but you need something powerful. Any motocross bike will do, perhaps with a few custom modifications – Evel Knievel favoured the Harley-Davidson XR-750, an 82 horsepower dirt-track racing bike, decorated with the stars and stripes of the American flag. Before you even start to think about your first jump, link up with the experts and learn everything you can from them. Get an experienced jumper to act as your mentor. You may even be able to find a stunt training centre in your area.

Be prepared to make many sacrifices in your search for this particular adrenalin rush. It is going to take a lot of your time and money, not to say emotional energy. Ideally, you want an employer and partner who understand your ambitions.

Start small: the current world record jump saw Australia's Robbie Maddison fly across 107 metres (351 ft) in Melbourne in 2008, but for you, that's a far-off dream. Your early jumps should be short and relatively unambitious – use them to get a sense of what you and your machine are capable of.

Any successful jump starts with calculations. With an expert, work out exactly what speed you need to be at when hitting the ramp to fly for your desired distance through the air. Always double- and triple-check your workings! Make sure you have all the relevant permissions to carry out a jump in any given location. Consider also the safety of your spectators – crash barriers are a good place to start.

Look after your bike – it needs to be in tip-top condition to take the force of a landing. Ensure there are no cracks in the frame, and pump your tyres to the optimum pressure. A padded seat might also prove a most telling investment. If any of the set-up is not exactly as you want it on the day, or if you are not feeling right yourself, then don't be ashamed to pull out. There's always another day – but there might not be if you push yourself into going ahead with a jump when you're not happy.

Make sure your ramps are perfectly aligned, and that you have a long enough run-up to achieve the desired speed. Before going for the jump itself, make some practice runs, pushing as close as you can to the point of no return. Think of it as the equivalent of a golfer practising a swing before teeing-off for real.

On your final approach, keep a careful eye on your approach speed – if it's not right, abort and reset yourself. Aim to hit the ramp straight on: you should be perching on the bike with your knees slightly bent and your body centrally balanced over the bike. Once on the ramp, press down on the handlebars to compress the forks, then decompress at the lip to provide an upward bounce as you lift off.

Keep the bike straight and balanced while in the air. The front wheel should be slightly raised, so that you land on the rear wheel first. As the front wheel hits the ground, keep it straight to avoid wobbles.

The rewards for jumping tend to come in the form of glory rather than cash – even the great Evel Knievel ruefully reflected that during his career he 'earned $60 million, spent $62 million'. Don't expect to get rich doing this, but make sure you get a big crowd in for your most daring feats so that you can at least soak up the adulation.

AIRBORNE *In 2010, Russian motorcyclist Alexey Kolesnikov completed the first ever motorcycle jump over a flying truck. Twelve metres (39.5 ft) separated the take-off and landing ramps, with Kolesnikov launching himself at a speed of 60 kilometres per hour (37 mph).*

89 | Perform on the flying trapeze

WHAT IT IS Soaring through the air beneath the Big Top
WHY YOU WON'T DO IT If the flying doesn't terrify you, then hitting the ground should

The flying trapeze act was made famous in the mid-19th century by the legendary Jules Léotard, and there's still no more spectacular sight beneath the Big Top than trapeze artists executing impossible tricks as they swing high in the air. So how can you, too, learn to 'fly through the air with the greatest of ease'?

Most modern trapeze acts include a flyer and a catcher, whose relationship needs to be underpinned by mutual trust. It can take years to reach performance standard, training for perhaps four hours a day, six days a week, but there's plenty of opportunity for novices to test their skills along the way. You'll need to be fit, extremely brave, prepared to take a few knocks and, obviously, you'll need a head for heights. You will likely be working at a height of 6–12 metres (20–40 ft) above the ground – high enough for any right-thinking person to demand a safety net (and a safety harness while you're learning). Léotard, working in the days before such equipment, laid out a series of mattresses in case of crash-landing.

Wear sensible sportswear – the spangly costume can come later. Grips made from tape are a valuable asset to protect your hands. Start by perfecting simply swinging from the bar. This is easier said than done – stepping off the platform for the first time is a true leap of faith. Try to stay calm – rub your hands with chalk to dry them and improve your grip, and

grasp the trapeze firmly in both hands. Aim to step off as if you were just going for a casual walk. This will provide you with a little initial momentum, which you can increase by swinging your legs. A more dramatic launch can cause the trapeze to tense suddenly, leaving you hanging in mid-air without momentum.

Once you've perfected the swing, you can start learning some simple manoeuvres and variant grips. Eventually you will be ready to work with a catcher. This essentially involves you letting go of your bar mid-swing and launching yourself into the grip of the catcher on the other bar (the 'catch trap'). Communication here is vital – the catcher will call to indicate they are ready to receive you, you will call to let them know you're on your way, and so on. Ultimately, the catcher will launch you back towards your trapeze (this is called a 'return'). All the while you will have the opportunity to entertain with any number of moves, from pirouettes and somersaults to 'angels' (when the catcher grips you by your feet and an arm).

Land a 747

WHAT IT IS Taking control of a jumbo jet
WHY YOU WON'T DO IT The average pilot has dedicated many years to learning the art

Despite what the movies might suggest, to date there are no recorded instances of untrained civilians safely landing a commercial aircraft in an emergency. In 2012 a passenger *did* help to land a 747 Jumbo Jet at Dublin airport after the first officer became ill – but that passenger just happened to be an off-duty pilot. But you never know – so what if you do find yourself unexpectedly on the flight deck?

One bit of advice that will serve you better than any other: don't panic! When you're trying to bring a flying tin can full of people safely out of the sky and back to the ground, a clear mind is your best friend. Ensure that any incapacitated members of the crew are not leaning on the controls, take a seat and buckle up.

Your first aim should be to get the aircraft on a stable path. On the instrument panel, there will be an attitude indicator (sometimes labelled 'artificial horizon' or 'gyro horizon'). This will tell you how the plane is oriented relative to the ground (the sky is a blue semicircle and the ground is brown, while the horizon is red), whether your wings (denoted by a pair of straight lines) are on an even keel, and if you're maintaining, gaining or losing height. A nearby altimeter should give your absolute height on a dial, but that can wait till later – the important question is whether the plane is flying straight and level. If the answer is yes, that's good – it probably

means that the autopilot is on and the computers are keeping the plane on the proverbial straight and narrow.

If, however, the plane's nose is pointing noticeably up or down, or if the wings seem to be doing their own thing, you'll need to get hold of the yoke (the big joystick-cum-steering-wheel that should be directly in front of you). Gently pull back to bring the nose up, push forward to descend, and pull to the left or right to balance the wings.

Once the immediate crisis is over, get professional help as soon as possible. Locate the hand-held radio, push the PTT (Press to Talk) button and say 'Mayday' three times. Then release the PTT button and await a response. If there is no immediate answer, set the radio frequency to 121.5 MHz. When you receive a response, explain your unenviable situation – make sure they understand that your previous aviation experience is limited to *Microsoft Flight Simulator*, and that you could do with a little bit of help.

expert will soon be on the line, working in unison with air traffic control to talk you through exactly what you need to do. In theory, it should now become a simple case of pushing the buttons and flicking the switches when they tell you to.

One of the many great things about modern jet airliners is that they can virtually land themselves, assuming the autopilot is on. The chances are that you will not have to do much at all until the plane is about 30 metres (100 ft) above the landing area. Locate the gear handle and engage the landing gear when you are told to. You will also be advised on how to adjust the slats and flaps to prepare for landing, and will need to manipulate the yoke as advised to bring the plane onto terra firma as smoothly as possible (though your passengers will probably forgive any stylistic shortcomings, given the circumstances).

Once you're safely on the ground, the next challenge is stopping. Pull the throttles all the way back and step on the brakes (found at the top of the rudder pedals at your feet). The rudder pedals are also likely to have some control over the nosewheel on the ground, so you can use them to steer your way down the central line if the plane appears to be veering off the runway.

TIN BIRD *The Boeing 747 'jumbo jet' first took to the skies in 1970, boasting far greater capacity than any previous passenger aircraft. Flying one remains the preserve of highly skilled and trained pilots, despite what a viewing of the movie* **Airplane!** *might suggest.*

Beneath the radio, there may be a transponder to help air traffic control to locate you. Set the dials to or type in the number '7700', which is a standard emergency call. An airport flight controller will do all they can to talk you through the steps to secure a safe landing. Listen to what they have to say and answer all their questions as accurately and concisely as possible. Don't get flustered. Ideally, a suitable

As the plane comes to a complete stop, you'll probably see the lights of emergency vehicles racing up the runway to meet you and hear the relieved cheering and applause from the passenger section. See if you can locate an 'ignition key' in front of you. Turn it to shut down the engine, unbuckle yourself from the seat and go and bask in your moment of glory.

91 Box with a kangaroo

WHAT IT IS Mixing it with a marsupial
WHY YOU WON'T DO IT Skippy never read the Queensberry Rules

The Australian Olympic movement uses an image of boxing kangaroo as its official mascot – it's a natural choice, considering that the 'roo is the country's most iconic animal, and its anthropomorphic boxing stance reflects the Aussie never-say-die attitude to sporting matters. But would you really want to take on one of these pugnacious marsupials in the ring?

Although some people dismiss the idea of boxing kangaroos as a modern myth or at least a misinterpretation of other behaviours, the fact of the matter is that kangaroos really do box. While both the males and females can spar, it is perhaps no great surprise that it is the male of the species (the buck) that most often partakes. While young joeys playfully bash each other about, among

ROO'D BEHAVIOUR
Two Western grey kangaroo males lay into each other in Western Australia. Males stand about 1.3 metres (4 ft 8 in) tall and can weigh more than 50 kilograms (110 lb). Fights break out as a way to establish social hierarchy within large kangaroo groups, as well as to assert mating rights over rival males.

adults it can be a rather more serious business, with contests frequently arising in order to establish the social hierarchy, to sort out territorial claims or simply to impress females. However, there is a vast gulf between these nature-driven engagements and the man-versus-beast contests of popular imagination.

Film footage from a hundred and more years ago – when animal rights were taken less seriously than today – shows men slugging it out against kangaroos who really did have their paws tied into boxing gloves, and despite the efforts of international animal welfare organizations, contests are still held in some parts of the world. In reality, however, kangaroos are largely peaceable creatures that do not go looking for trouble – and the last recorded case of a human being killed in a kangaroo attack was in 1936.

Nonetheless, it is not out of the question that you might find yourself unexpectedly pitted against a kangaroo in the wild. In 2010, for instance, jogger David Striegl was attacked from behind while running on Mount Ainslie near Canberra – a single smack to the head was enough to knock him out cold. The motivation for the attack was never established: it could be that he inadvertently looked at the kangaroo the wrong way, but the animal was probably responding to a perceived encroachment on its territory.

So what can you do to emerge from a brush-up mostly intact? Firstly, try not to antagonize the animal. There are three principal reasons why one is likely to get annoyed with you: if it sees you as a threat to its territory, if it thinks you are muscling in on its mates, or if it suspects that you are withholding food.

Read the signals: an aggressive kangaroo will raise itself up, arch its back and tense its muscles. Pulling up grass is another tactic used to intimidate rivals. The aggressor may also go in for a bit of shadow boxing, and in the wild will grab an opponent by the throat to commence a scuffle. If you spot any of these signs, attempt to defuse the situation. Keep your distance if possible, and try to put a barrier between you and the animal – even holding a large branch against you can help. Try to make a slow retreat, but don't try to outrun the 'roo – when it catches you up (and it will) you will be at your most vulnerable. Displaying submissiveness can also deflect a tussle (even if it dents your pride): avoid eye contact, assume a crouching position and let out a short, low grunt to admit defeat.

If it comes to a fight, your chances of defeating a kangaroo in close combat are not good. Of all the kangaroo breeds, the largest is the red kangaroo, which can be up to 2 metres (6 ft 8 in) tall and 90 kilograms (200 lb) in weight. They can give you a nasty swipe with their front paws, but it is the powerful hind legs that are really dangerous. Using their tails for balance, they will kick at your abdomen with claws sharp enough to disembowel.

Aim for self-preservation. Protect your face and vital organs as best you can. Turning your body sideways will offer a narrower target to your assailant. Even better is to roll into a ball and hope the kangaroo eventually gets bored and goes home.

HAVING A POP *Better known in Britain these days as a sober commentator on pop history, former BBC Radio One disc jockey Paul Gambaccini somehow found himself on the wrong end of a boxing contest with a kangaroo at a circus in Eastbourne, England, in the summer of 1980.*

92 Play Russian Roulette

WHAT IT IS A game that puts your life at stake
WHY YOU WON'T DO IT Because it's illegal and stupid – and fortune doesn't favour the foolish

Calling Russian Roulette a game is rather like calling Niagara Falls a 'discreet water feature' or describing a trek to the South Pole as a 'bracing walk'. This is truly a game with no winner so if you're tempted to have a go, we strongly advise you stick with reading about it instead.

It's unclear who first came up with the idea of Russian Roulette, but it makes its first definite appearance in a short story from 1937 by Swiss writer Georges Surdez. Some say Surdez invented the whole thing, but in the story Surdez claimed it was a game played among Russian soldiers in Romania during the First World War. Author Graham Greene claimed to have played in his youth (which would predate Surdez's writing, if not his proposed origin story itself.

Over the years, this deadly game has exerted a strange fascination – blues star Johnny Ace died during a game in 1954. Finnish magician Aimo Lekas shot himself dead on stage while performing a (poorly planned!) Russian Roulette routine in 1975, and as recently as 2012, slamball player Dion Mays killed himself in a game in California.

So how is it 'played'? It requires between two and six participants, and a six chamber revolver. A live round is put into one chamber. The cylinder is spun so that no one knows where the live round

is, and 'players' take it in turns to place the muzzle against their temples and pull the trigger. Assuming they don't die, the gun moves on to the next participant. In one variant, the chamber is spun only once so that the longer a player continues, the less chance he or she has of surviving. In another, the chamber is spun before each shot, keeping the odds of survival that little bit higher.

Still, the odds don't look great. In the second variant, players have a 1 in 6 (or 17 per cent) chance of dying with each shot. In the first, the odds creep steadily higher, until if everyone else has survived Player 6 is guaranteed to die.

The game is illegal throughout the world and those who perish while competing are generally classified as suicides. Academic studies reveal that the average player is male, under 30 and under the influence of alcohol or drugs. If you feel the need to do something reckless in that kind of situation, why not stick to texting an ex at three in the morning or buying something inadvisable on eBay?

93

Become a chess grandmaster

WHAT IT IS Proving yourself at the ultimate game of tactics

WHY YOU WON'T DO IT The game has consumed some of the sharpest minds of our age

The title of grandmaster is awarded to only the highest rated chess players in the world by the game's governing body, the Fédération Internationale des Échecs (FIDE). Today there are about a thousand grandmasters around the world – if you want to become one of them, you'll need natural talent and a lot of practice.

Although the term was informally in use as early as 1907, it was not until 1950 that FIDE officiallfy named its first 27 grandmasters. The criteria for qualification have gone through several revisions over the years, and the modern system is based on proposals suggested by Dr Wilfried Dorazil in 1970. To become a grandmaster you need to achieve an 'Elo' player rating of more than 2,500, and at least two 'grandmaster norm' results from a total of 27 games in tournaments involving other grandmasters.

Assuming you have got to grips with the basics of the game, and have even got the edge over a computerized opponent, then a local chess club will help take your game to the next level. Think about getting a specialist instructor with some first-hand experience of the FIDE tournament scene and an Elo score of 1,800 or above.

Immerse yourself in the game. Play as often as you can against opponents who can beat you, as they are the ones from whom you will learn most. Go and watch others playing at tournaments as well. This will improve your knowledge of tactics and will also familiarize you with potential opponents.

Study, study, study. You need to become a master of all aspects of the game – openings, middle games and end games. There are thousands upon thousands of scenarios that you might meet in a long career, and it will take a lot of time to get to grips with even a fraction of them. For instance, Garry Kasparov, one of the greatest players of all time (shown opposite) is said to have a memory bank of some 300,000 openings.

The game is as much about analysing what your opponent is thinking as much as formulating your own plans. Chess is psychological war and the victor will be the one who stays calms and collected. Panic and mistakes go hand in hand. If you're mastering chess, you probably won't have time to play much poker but make sure you work on your poker face at least. Don't let a slack facial expression give you away!

94

Walk a tightrope

WHAT IT IS A casual stroll above the jaws of doom
WHY YOU WON'T DO IT There is no margin for error

Also known as funambulism, tightrope walking is a skill that tests your balance, coordination and head for heights. It also seems to have a natural attraction for eccentrics – consider Charles Blondin, perhaps the most famous funambulist of all, who once stopped to cook an omelette while on a rope above Niagara Falls...

There are three major categories of funambulism:
• The slackwire, a low-tension wire on which performers generally practise balancing tricks or juggling.
• The tightwire, a high-tension wire kept relatively low to the ground, on which the tightrope walker performs dance steps and acrobatic tricks.
• The highwire, the classic tightrope act, utilizing a high-tension wire usually at least 6 metres (20 ft) above the ground, for acrobatics and other stunts.

Find a professional to train with – you should ensure you have a good basic level of fitness before you begin. Stilt-walking is a good way to develop your balance, as is walking along a low-level balance beam. While training, make full use of harnesses and safety nets, and always work with a partner who can come to your rescue. When you are ready to move up to a rope, begin with the slightly more forgiving slackrope, and fix it just a few inches from the floor to ease the pain of inevitable falls. Don't try to walk until you have first mastered

simply standing still. Many people find it easier to start midway along the rope rather than at one end. When you step on to the rope, look ahead, not down. Focus on balancing through your hips and use your arms to keep you steady. Carry a pole to help you maintain equilibrium. When standing on two legs, keep your weight on the back leg. Now try to stand on one leg, which will ultimately give you more freedom of movement.

When you're ready to start walking, do so confidently. Take a single step, and then resume standing until you're ready for the next step. Keep your centre of mass over the wire at all times. When you have mastered walking, try turning by shifting your weight from one foot to the other (with the second foot at right angles to the first), then pivoting on the ball of your first foot. As you grow in confidence, make the tightrope tauter and raise it higher. And if you need inspiration, try watching *Man on Wire*, a spellbinding documentary following Philippe Petit's 1974 walk between the Twin Towers of the New York World Trade Center.

95 Tame a lion

WHAT IT IS Establishing mastery over the king of the jungle
WHY YOU WON'T DO IT This isn't a friendly tabby we're dealing with here

The classic image of the lion tamer is one of a man in top hat and red tails, cracking a whip and wielding a chair while the king of the beasts does his bidding, in front of a baying crowd beneath the Big Top. Indeed, there was a time when this would have been a pretty accurate representation – today, though, lion taming is much more concerned with building bonds of trust.

The first recognized lion tamer was a Frenchman, Henri Martin, who worked in the early part of the 19th century. A retired horse trainer, his act initially used tigers and only later lions. In some ways he was quite a modern performer, teaching the animals to obey simple instructions after spending much time building up a strong degree of familiarity and trust.

Unfortunately, the act was then developed into the classic 'whip and chair' performance by the likes of the Americans Isaac van Amburgh (who emerged onto the scene in 1833) and Clyde Beatty, who brought lion taming to the silver screen in the 1930s. These performers were more concerned with dominating the animals – indeed, van Amburgh is said to have beaten his animals with a crowbar while Beatty performed with a pistol.

Happily, such approaches are now off the agenda: animal rights have come to the fore, and today, most practitioners firmly define themselves as 'trainers' rather than 'tamers'. Even so, some animal rights groups argue that such acts are unjustifiable in the modern age.

A lion has claws up to 7.5 centimetre (3 in) long and a jaw that can lock itself round your head. For those reasons alone, they should always be treated with respect. Any animals you end up performing with are likely to have been born in captivity, but that doesn't make them any less dangerous. The key to a successful act is experience, which must be built up over a long period. You will need patience and dedication. This is not the sort of thing you can wing on the day, and theory is no match for real face-to-face exposure. As the famed Greek conductor, Dimitri Mitropoulos, once put it: 'I never use a score when conducting my orchestra. Does a lion tamer enter a cage with a book on how to tame a lion?'

Nevertheless, it's also worth taking time to study the animals academically. Consider taking a course in zoology, veterinary science or an associated subject. Anything that helps you better

HERE KITTY, KITTY *Previous page: British lion trainer Martin Lacey Jr entertains the crowd at the 34th International Circus Festival in Monte Carlo, Monaco, in 2010. Above: The art has a long heritage. Here a performer is seen at the centre of his pride in a photo dating from around 1890.*

Once you get to a point of familiarity and peaceful coexistence with your new feline friend, you can start to think about how to develop an act. Aside from the danger and unpredictability involved, teaching a lion to follow your instructions is not too different from training any other animal, and involves a process of repetition and positive reinforcement (more often than not in the form of food).

For instance, if you want the lion to turn in a clockwise circle at the click of your fingers, it needs to learn that your clicking is its cue. Every time the lion turns in the right direction when you click, reward it with a treat. The lion eventually learns that your click is its cue to spin, and then results in a reward.

When working with such potentially deadly wild animals, you must be sure to maintain your focus at all times. However skilled you are, lion taming is always dangerous and lion tamers will rue the day they become complacent. Even the best can be at risk – German-American duo Siegfried and Roy were the stars of the most famous big cat show in the world, at the MGM Mirage casino in Las Vegas, and among the most highly paid people in the entertainment industry, until Roy Horn was badly mauled by a tiger called Montecore during a show in 2003. The cause of the animal's sudden attack has never been satisfactorily established – one theory is that Montecore was actually attempting to pull Horn to safety after he slipped and fell. Once Horn had recovered the duo went on to perform wth it on several more occasions before their eventual retirement.

But it just goes to prove that even the most expertly trained animals retain a wild and unpredictable streak. When you work with a big cat, that should always be your uppermost thought.

understand how lions live and think is invaluable. Volunteer at a zoo or a safari park so that you can start to interact with the animals.

When you begin learning to 'tame', work with an old hand who can advise and guide you. An expert will instruct you on how to build up trust between you and the lion until you can safely inhabit the same space. Needless to say, you won't be able to walk straight into the lion's enclosure on Day One – and if you try, you're unlikely to be walking back out again.

Walk on water

WHAT IT IS Keeping your feet as well as your head above water
WHY YOU WON'T DO IT It is an occupation best practised by deities

Ever since the the gospel tales of Jesus Christ miraculously walking on water, it has been a metaphor for virtually any apparently impossible act. Though the internet is awash with clips of humans seemingly defying the laws of physics to traverse lakes and rivers, none has so far proved anything more than a hoax. But with a little bit of science, you too could at least appear to achieve the impossible...

The idea of being able to walk on water has long fascinated humans, with the concept appearing in a number of classical and religious texts. Even Leonardo da Vinci sketched out an idea for a system of floats that could be worn on the feet to allow travel across the water's surface. Sadly, though, the brutal facts of biology mediate against us ever accomplishing such a thing without artificial aid – we simply weigh too much, and all our mass pushes down through our relatively small feet, resulting in a lot of pressure that ensures we get that sinking feeling.

Nevertheless, there are several animal species that can walk on water. One of the most interesting is the common basilisk *Basilicus basilicus*, a lizard hailing from Central and South America that is somewhat irreverently nicknamed the Jesus lizard. It can run across water for distance of several metres, avoiding the wet stuff by rapidly slapping its feet on the water's surface, to provide lift and create air cavities which they have moved on from before they can close up.

The lizard will take as many as 20 steps per second to keep up momentum. For humans to replicate this, we'd need giant feet that we could bring up to our ears in order to create sufficient 'slap'.

But fortunately there is an alternative: cornflour. By adding sufficient amounts of this common thickening agent to water (and it does take a lot), you can create a 'non-Newtonian' liquid that doesn't behave like normal water. Now, if the surface of the water is hit hard enough, particles in the water group together momentarily to make the surface hard. Move quickly enough and put enough force into each step, and you really can walk across the surface of a sufficiently dense cornflour solution. If you have a sweet tooth, then you could achieve a similar effect using custard.

Fun though all this may sound, it's still rather messy and better read about in theory than demonstrated in practice. If you must do it, then keep the water wings handy in case you start to sink – and have a shower afterwards!

97 **Find the Holy Grail**

WHAT IT IS The last word
in treasure hunts
WHY YOU WON'T DO IT
Many intrepid adventurers
have failed in the quest
before you

The Holy Grail has fascinated us for the best part of a thousand years
and provided the object of countless heroic quests from the legends of
King Arthur to *The Da Vinci Code*. But despite experts disagreeing even
on basics such as what a grail is, there's no shortage of candidates and
possible locations.

The Holy Grail legend is widely thought
to be an amalgam of Christian and Celtic
traditions, and first took form in an epic
poem written by Frenchman Chrétien de
Troyes in the late 12th century. It tells the
story of Perceval, a Welsh knight, who
comes upon the grail when dining at the
castle of the mysterious Fisher King. It
contains a single communion wafer that
miraculously provides sustenance for the
Fisher King's sick father. A little later,
the grail's back-story was developed in
the work of Robert de Boron. His tale has
Joseph of Arimathea collecting Christ's
blood in the grail as Jesus was being
crucified. Joseph then has the grail sent
to Britain for safekeeping, and King
Arthur and his knights go in search of
it. So how might you succeed where the
knights of the Round Table failed?

Firstly, you will need to establish in
your own mind just what the grail is.
Traditionally, it was a vessel (some say
a cup, others a plate or bowl) used by
Christ at the Last Supper. In more recent
times, some have seen the grail as a
metaphor. For instance, (spoiler alert!)

The Da Vinci Code reworks the idea that
Mary Magdalene is the grail – recipient
of the holy bloodline after marrying and
having children with Jesus. Whatever
your choice, it will be based on faith and
instinct rather than concrete evidence.

Most legends suggest the true grail can
only be recognized and found by a wise,
heroic figure, so if that sounds like you,
decide where you're going to start your
search. Famous grail candidates include:
• The Antioch Chalice, found in Antioch
in modern-day Turkey in 1911 and
now in the possession of the New York
Metropolitan Museum of Art.
• The Jerusalem Chalice, a silver cup
described by an Anglo-Saxon pilgrim in
the seventh century but never found.
• The Genoa Chalice, located in Genoa
Cathedral, and crafted in Egyptian glass.
• The Valencia Chalice, a red agate
vessel displayed in Valencia Cathedral
(shown opposite).
• Other theories have it buried beneath
Rosslyn Chapel in Scotland, while
Glastonbury Tor in Somerset, southwest
England, is yet another possibility.

98 Perform the Indian rope trick

WHAT IT IS Climbing up a rope that is suspended in thin air

WHY YOU WON'T DO IT This legendary illusion might never have happened as it is classically described

Travellers to the East have been bringing back tales of tricks similar to the Indian rope trick since at least the 14th century, although the earliest reports involve a chain rather than a rope. However, the trick in all its gory detail seems to have been nothing but a journalist's hoax dating to the late Victorian period, and there's little to suggest it's ever actually been performed.

It was in 1890 that journalist John Elbert Wilkie provided the first full report of the Indian rope trick, in a pseudonymous piece for the *Chicago Tribune*. Despite the paper's own later admission that his article was a hoax, the trick fired the public imagination, and by 1934 the Magic Circle of London was offering a princely reward of 500 guineas for anyone able to perform the illusion.

The full version of the trick starts with the magician displaying a large basket containing a coil of ordinary rope. He hurls the rope into the air, whereupon it magically hangs, seemingly suspended from above. A young assistant now shins up the rope, climbing higher and higher until he disappears from view. The magician now calls his accomplice back to the ground, and when there is no response, he becomes angry and follows the boy up the rope, producing a knife as he climbs. He too disappears, and amid the boy's blood-curdling screams. the boy's body parts rain from above. The magician now returns, and the rope collapses when he reaches the ground.

He gathers up the body parts, puts them in the basket and covers them with a cloth. At the magician's command the boy reappears, miraculously whole again.

So how might the trick be done? Some claim it requires mastery of levitation or other genuinely magical powers, while others suggest mass hypnosis. Sceptics believe the trick could be done in poor light with a system of support wires suspended between nearby posts or trees. But what of the dismembered and resurrected assistant? Wilder suppositions include the use of twins, with one sacrificed in each performance!

Perhaps the truth is that the trick simply can't be done, and never existed in its complete form. But in 1995 Ishamuddin Khan, a resident of the Delhi slums, did perform a version of sorts, propelling what witnesses confirmed as an ordinary rope into the air to a height of 6 metres (20 ft), and allowing a young audience member to climb it. This remarkable feat was captured on video, and has yet to be adequately explained.

Wing-walk

WHAT IT IS A vertigo-inducing mix of acrobatics and aerobatics
WHY YOU WON'T DO IT While adrenalin junkies can buy a taste of the experience, it takes years of training to go beyond simply standing there

For those of us who come out in cold sweats at the mere thought of sitting in a jumbo jet, the idea of being strapped to the wings of a plane, exposed to the raw elements as it sweeps and loops and whooshes through an aerobatic display, is simply terrifying. Can there be many pastimes more insane? Probably not.

The art of wing-walking is generally accepted to have been invented by an American, Ormer Locklear, who had signed up with the Army Air Service during the First World War. In that age of the biplane, mechanical faults were reasonably common mid-flight and Locklear took to fixing them by extricating himself from his cockpit and climbing onto the wings while still up in the air. As other airmen followed his lead, they pushed each other on to ever more extreme exhibitions of showmanship. By the 1920s there was a thriving industry centred around their exploits at air shows and barnstorms.

However, danger was always close at hand. Locklear himself, having become a stuntman in Hollywood, died in an accident in 1920. In later decades the practice was heavily regulated and at times even banned on both sides of the Atlantic but these days you can have a go in the knowledge that safety standards are exacting. As long as you are fit, healthy and game, you can become part of your own aerobatic spectacular.

But keep your expectations realistic – gone are the days of parading up and down the wings, hanging by your teeth and leaping from plane to plane. Now wing-walkers are required to be fixed to a rig. The most talented can still perform tricks such as handstands, but most participants have to settle for standing there and throwing the odd pose.

You don't need to be an Olympian to participate but consider whether you are physically suitable. You need to have decent levels of strength, balance, flexibility, agility and coordination to manoeuvre yourself onto the plane in the first place and then cope with flying at speeds in excess of 160 kilometres per hour (100 mph). If you suffer from certain ailments or injuries, you will be ruled out altogether. For instance, wing-walking is not suitable for those suffering from epilepsy, head injuries, diabetes, heart problems, dislocations, mental illness or addiction. Most companies also have strict height and weight restrictions. And they will require you to sign a disclaimer in the event of something going wrong!

FORE! *Once you're safely up in the air, there are any number of opportunities for additional stunts. Al Wilson became the first (and seemingly only) man to drive a golf ball from the wings of an aeroplane in flight. Born in 1895, he was a stunt pilot who featuredin a succession of early movies until his death in an air show in 1932.*

Age, on the other hand, is no barrier. In 2009 a nine-year-old by the name of Tiger Brewer wing-walked over Gloucestershire in England. The following year, another Briton, Tom Lackey, became the oldest recorded participant at the age of 90.

Work with the experts. There are numerous professional display teams who offer training courses and will ensure you are armed with all the right knowledge and equipment. You can be in the air after just a morning's training, during which you will be taught essentials such as how the rig and harness work and what hand signals you'll use to communicate with the pilot.

Make sure you're wearing the right garb – things get very cold when you're up in the air, so wear a couple of layers of loose-fitting clothes. Opt for flat-soled lace-up shoes (no high heels, please). Invest in some earplugs and goggles but leave your jewellery at home.

Once you've been strapped in, relax your back into the rig and be prepared to experience some curious sensations. During moves such as the 'zoom climb' and the 'run and break', you are likely to experience facial contortions. In addition, not to put too fine a point on it, if you have any snot to escape, it will! Getting the odd fly stuck in your teeth is another unpleasant occupational hazard, and if it rains, you'll likely be pelted with ice pellets at high altitude (which normally melt before they hit the ground). So prepare for a split lip – no one ever said this would make you look beautiful.

Escape from Alcatraz

Between 1934 and 1963, an outcrop sitting 2.5 kilometres (1.5 miles) out in San Francisco Bay, was the home of a federal prison from which no one is known to have successfully escaped. Should they reopen the prison and you're unlucky enough to find yourself incarcerated there, you might want to follow the example of three jailbirds who might just have made it to freedom.

The Rock, as Alcatraz is also known, played host to a lighthouse, a military garrison and a military prison before it became a federal prison. Among its most famous inmates were Al Capone and Robert Franklin Stroud (the 'Birdman of Alcatraz' immortalized in the film of the same name). These days, a ferry that leaves from the city's Pier 33 will take law-abiding tourists back and forth to Alcatraz as often as they wish.

Some 36 prisoners are known to have attempted a break-out from the prison's confines in 14 separate incidents (sadly, despite the claims of the 1996 movie *The Rock*, Sean Connery was not among them). The most violent attempt, in 1946, resulted in the Battle of Alcatraz, a two-day gun battle that left three prisoners and two warders dead.

Arguably the greatest escape attempt, however, was that made by Frank Morris and two brothers, John and Clarence Anglin, in June 1962. These three definitely made it off the island and into the water, and were never seen again.

The official line is that they must have fallen victim to the bay's dangerous currents, but there have always been stories that they succeeded in swimming across to San Francisco and starting new lives as free men. Regardless of their eventual fate, their escape plan was a remarkable example of ingenuity, patience and endurance – it inspired the 1979 Clint Eastwood movie *Escape from Alcatraz*, and has echoes in a rather more famous prison-escape story – *The Shawshank Redemption*. If you want to follow in their footsteps, then this is what you do:

• Fashion your tools out of the sight of guards. Use whatever comes to hand – Morris and the Anglins made a spoon by soldering the metal from a dime coin, and fashioned a drill from an old vacuum cleaner motor. This takes both patience and ingenuity – if you're planning on attempting this kind of escpe, then you might want to take some sort of night class while you are still at liberty.

• Get yourself assigned to a cell in a suitable part of the prison (Cell Block B

Model industries building

Laundry

Recreation yard

Main Cellhouse

Lighthouse

Apartments

Officer's club

Dock

Helipad

NO WAY OUT *An aerial view of the infamous prison at Alcatraz – once home to some of America's most infamous prisoners. The Rock has not served as a penitentiary for more than half a century, and in 1986 it was designated a National Historic Landmark.*

CALIFORNIA

ALCATRAZ

Golden Gate Bridge

Berkeley

Oakland

Pacific Ocean

SAN FRANCISCO

San Francisco Bay

INSIDE THE BIG HOUSE *A view down the main corridor of one of Alcatraz's cell houses. The institution's longest-serving prisoner was Alvin 'Creepy' Karpis, a gangster and one-time Public Enemy Number One. Convicted of robbery, kidnap and murder, he spent some 26 years on The Rock (shown opposite).*

is ideal), locate an air vent and begin to scrape away the concrete around the protective grille using the tools you've made. Again, patience here is the key. The work might also be noisy – the 1962 escapees disguised the sound by working during the prison's allotted music hour, and loudly playing the accordion throughout.

• When you are able to detach the grille, replace its metal rivets with fakes fashioned out of soap so that you can remove and replace it speedily without raising the suspicions of the guards.

• Prepare a papier-mâché dummy, complete with hair smuggled from the prison barbers, and position it in your bed so that any passing guards will be fooled.

• At an agreed time, remove the grille, enter the utility shaft and make your way onto the prison roof. It's worth checking that all of your fellow escapees have gathered there before embarking on the next stage – Morris and the Anglins crucially forgot this, leaving a fourth cohort, Allen West, stuck in his cell and left to face the music.

• Climb down the outside of the building and make your way to the northeast shore. Using your prison-issue raincoats, fashion yourself a raft.

• Paddle like crazy and be prepared to get wet and swim for it!

Assuming you haven't drowned (or been shot at by a vigilant guard), disappear into the crowds of San Francisco and live a little. And try to stay on the straight and narrow this time.

Index

Acknowledgements

This book would not have been possible were it not for a host of experts, far too numerous to mention here, who have been prepared to share their knowledge and experience of their particular fields of expertise.

Thanks also to my agent, James Wills, as well as Richard Green, Kerry Enzor and the rest of the team at Quercus. Also to Giles Sparrow and Tim Brown at Pikaia, to whom I am very grateful for making this book look as good as it does. And a final thanks, as ever, to Rosie.

For Matt and Amy

Picture credits

The following abbreviations are used throughout the picture credits:
t = top, b = bottom, l = left, r = right, c = centre.

2-3: KPA/Zuma/Rex Features; 6tl: © Ocean/Corbis; tr: © John Van Hasselt/Sygma/Corbis; 7tl: AFP/Getty Images; tr: NASA/Science Photo Library; 8tl: © Ali Haider/epa/Corbis; tr: Rex Features; 9tl: © Chad Ehlers / Alamy; tr: © Ali Haider/epa/Corbis; 11: Luca Bruno, Associated Press; 13: © Claro Cortes IV/Reuters/Corbis; 14: © Iain Masterton / Alamy; 16: © James Marshall/Corbis; 17: Greg Elms; 19: Getty Images; 21: © Ali Haider/epa/Corbis; 22: © Fadi Al-Assaad/Reuters/Corbis; 24: © Corbis; 25: © John Van Hasselt/Sygma/Corbis; 27: Mark J Terrill/Associated Press; 28: AFP/Getty Images; 30: Newspix/Rex Features; 33: AFP/Getty Images; 34-5: AFP/Getty Images; 35: AFP/Getty Images; 37: Barcroft Media via Getty Images; 39: WireImage; 41: © Robert Harding Picture Library Ltd / Alamy; 43: Gilles Levent/Rex Features; 44: Manu Fernandez/Associated Press; 47: © Caroline Cortizo / Alamy; 48: AFP/Getty Images; 50: © Ocean/Corbis; 51: © Bettmann/Corbis; 53: © Anthony Sambuco/Demotix/Corbis; 55t: © Kenneth Johansson/Corbis; 55b: PlanetObserver/Science Photo Library; 57: Hôtel Président Wilson; 59: © Zainal abd Halim/Reuters/Corbis; 61: © Purcell Team / Alamy; 63: © Bettmann/Corbis; 65: Associated Press; 66: Rex Features; 67: Copyright Bettmann/Corbis / AP Images; 68-9: KeystoneUSA-Zuma/Rex Features; 71: AFP/Getty Images; 73: © Jim McHugh/Sygma/Corbis; 75: Andrey Bayda /Shutterstock; 77: © John Lund/Drew Kelly/Blend Images/Corbis; 79: © InterFoto / Alamy; 81: Getty Images; 82: © Yves Forestier/Sygma/Corbis; 83: Paul Raffaele/Rex Features; 85: © Yann Arthus-Bertrand/Corbis; 86-7: © Def Vid/Demotix/Corbis; 89: Lehtikuva OY/Rex Features; 90: © Julian Parker / Alamy; 92-3: KeystoneUSA-Zuma/Rex Features; 95: © Chad Ehlers / Alamy; 97: Rex Features; 98: © Corbis; 101: InterFoto / Sammlung Rauch / Mary Evans; 103: © National Geographic Image Collection / Alamy; 105: © Bob Treheurne / Alamy; 107: © Yann Arthus-Bertrand/Corbis; 109: © Bettmann/Corbis; 111: © Tim Thompson/Corbis; 112: © Accent Alaska.com / Alamy; 115: © Roger Ressmeyer/Corbis; 117: Mehau Kulyk/Science Photo Library; 119: Steve Gschmeissner/Science Photo Library; 120: James King-Holmes/Science Photo Library; 122: Everett Collection/Rex Features; 123: Associated Press; 125: © Keren Su/Corbis; 127: Getty Images; 129: Mark Wilson; 131: © Roland Seitre / naturepl.com; 133: © Stefano Bianchetti/Corbis; 134: Press Association; 137: OceanPhoto/FLPA; 138: © Wolfgang Kaehler/Corbis;

141: Jeffrey Coolidge; 143: Mills/Hulton Archive/Getty; 144: Jon Santa Cruz/Rex Features; 146: NASA, ESA, and P. Kalas (University of California, Berkeley and SETI Institute); 147: Detlev van Ravenswaay/Science Photo Library; 149: Crafty Dogma via Flickr; 151: © Heritage Images/Corbis; 153: Gerben Oppermans/Getty; 155: © TopFoto; 156: © Jessica Rinaldi/Reuters/Corbis; 157: Detlev vam Ravenswaay/Science Photo Library; 158: Everett Collection/Rex Features; 161: © 1999 Credit:Topham Picturepoint; 163: AP Images; 166: Getty Images; 169: Rex Features; 171: Getty Images; 173: Barcroft Media via Getty Images; 174: © Time Images / Alamy; 176: Time & Life Pictures/Getty Images; 179: Maximilien Brice, Cern/Science Photo Library; 180: © 2009 CERN; 182: NASA; 183: NASA/Science Photo Library; 185: © Jessica Garland / Alamy; 186: © Radius Images / Alamy; 187: © Laperruque / Alamy; 188-9: © Corbis; 191: © The Art Archive / Alamy; 193: Taxi/Mike Owen/Getty; 195: Rolf Bruderer; 197: © Cultura Creative / Alamy; 199 t& b: © Bettmann/Corbis; 201: NASA/Science Photo Library; 203: © Bernd Vogel/Corbis; 204: © Bettmann/Corbis; 206: © Bettmann/Corbis; 207: © Wayne Hutchinson / Alamy; 211: KeystoneUSA-Zuma/Rex Features; 212: Red Bull Content Pool/Rex Features; 214: KeystoneUSA-Zuma/Rex Features; 215: Sipa Press/Rex Features; 217: Peter Brooker/Rex Features; 218: © Steve Vidler / Alamy; 220-1: Sipa Press/Rex Features; 223: © Jane Hobson / Alamy; 225: © Fredrik von Erichsen/dpa/Corbis; 226: © Jid Webb / Alamy; 227: Auscape / UIG; 228: Getty Images; 231: © Photos 12 / Alamy; 233: © Louie Psihoyos/Corbis; 235: Tyler Stableford; 237: AFP/Getty Images; 238: Copyright Bettmann/Corbis / AP Images; 241: Gonzalo Azumendi; 243: © 2004 Credit:TopFoto; 245: Rror/Wikipedia; 246: © Bettmann/Corbis; 248t: © David R. Frazier Photolibrary, Inc. / Alamy; 248b: PlanetObserver/Science Photo Library; 249: Andrea Pistolesi;

Illustrations on pages 31, 92 (bottom), 177 and 209 by Glyn Walton
Illustration on page 114 by Tim Brown

Quercus Editions Ltd
55 Baker Street
7th floor, South Block
London
W1U 8EW

First published in 2013

Copyright © 2013 Quercus Editions Ltd

All rights reserved. No part of this publication may
be reproduced, stored in a retrieval system, or
transmitted in any form or by any means, electronic,
mechanical, photocopying, recording, or otherwise,
without the prior permission in writing of the
copyright owner and publisher.

The picture credits constitute an extension to this
copyright notice.

Every effort has been made to contact copyright
holders. However, the publishers will be glad to
rectify in future editions any inadvertent omissions
brought to their attention.

Quercus Editions Ltd hereby exclude all liability to the
extent permitted by law for any errors or omissions
in this book and for any loss, damage or expense
(whether direct or indirect) suffered by a third party
relying on any information contained in this book.

A catalogue record of this book is available from the
British Library

UK and associated territories: ISBN 978 1 78206 455 8

Printed and bound in China

10 9 8 7 6 5 4 3 2 1